ANDY'S GAME

THE INSIDE STORY OF THE
WORLD CUP

ANDY'S GAME

THE INSIDE STORY OF THE
WORLD CUP

ANDY TOWNSEND

WITH PAUL KIMMAGE

STANLEY PAUL

First published 1994

1 3 5 7 9 10 8 6 4 2

Copyright © Andy Townsend 1994

Andy Townsend has asserted his right under the
Copyright, Designs and Patents Act 1988 to be identified
as the author of this work

First published in the United Kingdom in 1994
by Stanley Paul & Co. Ltd
Random House, 20 Vauxhall Bridge Road
London SW1V 2SA

Random House Australia (Pty) Limited
20 Alfred Street, Milsons Point, Sydney
New South Wales 2061, Australia

Random House New Zealand Limited
19 Poland Road, Glenfield
Auckland 10, New Zealand

Random House South Africa (Pty) Limited
PO Box 337, Bergvlei, South Africa

Random House UK Limited Reg. No. 954009

A CIP catalogue record for this book is available
from the British Library

ISBN 0 09 179012 3

Design & make up Roger Walker/Graham Harmer

Printed and bound in Great Britain by
Clays Ltd, St Ives plc

PHOTOGRAPH ACKNOWLEDGEMENTS

The author and publisher would like to thank Billy Stickland/INPHO,
Don Townsend, and Conrad Hafenrichter/*Sunday Magazine*
for allowing the use of copyright photographs.

Contents

Dedication

For Jackie, Daniel and Kelly,
my family, friends and all those
who have supported me over the years...
and a special mention for Bridgid Browne,
without whom this book would have been rather 'thin'

Prologue

PART 1:

LONG NIGHTS AT SOUTHAMPTON...
THE TROUBLE WITH JIMMY

eeeeaarrrryyoo....

I squint through an eye.... That sound, a groaning, coming from somewhere downstairs. I try lifting my head... the pillow feels good.... Tired, so tired... such a long day... the match, the drive back to Southampton, the meal at the Chinese, the couple of beers, the chat with Jimmy... Jimmy! Where's Jimmy? My head is numb, fuzzy, spinning. That noise again. I should get up....

eeeeaarrrryyoo....

'Come back and stay in my place,' I had suggested. A bad mistake. Jimmy's a thinker, a talker, likes to delve really deeply into life's great mysteries. At two o' clock you listen. At three it's getting hard... at four your eyes are closing and you decide you've had enough. 'Sorry, Jim, I'm knackered mate. I'm off to bed.'

'Sit down,' he says. 'I'm not finished.' He blocks the stairs. We open a bottle – one for the road. He talks some more about football, about life. Deep, so deep. Tired, so tired. 'Jim, get out of my way, mate. See you in the morning. I'm off bed.'

eeeeaaaarrryyooo...

But that sound, that groaning, coming from somewhere downstairs... vague, yet strangely familiar.

The day, a Saturday, had started with a game. A League game. A 7–0 trouncing on the plastic at Luton. We were awful, the manager was seething. 'Everyone on the coach, meeting tomorrow morning,' he growled. Which was a pity. I hadn't planned going home on the coach. Jackie had just found out she was pregnant and we wanted to drive straight to our parents in London after the game. Not now. Not after 7–0. She drove on to her mother's and I returned to Southampton with the rest of the team. On the coach, I got talking to Jimmy. Great fellow Jimmy, one of my favourite people at the club. We go for a beer. Then

a late-night meal at the usual haunt in Southampton – the Happy Talk
Chinese. Given my company, the name is fairly appropriate.

Although he was one of the great unsung heroes at Liverpool, where
he won League and European titles, I wasn't sure about Jimmy Case
when he first signed from Brighton. He was a rival, you see – played
central midfield. And even though the transfer fee was minimal
(£20,000), when you are young and trying to break through you worry
about these things.

There was also his manner. He had this very peculiar way. 'I don't
know about you, son,' he'd say out of the blue after a game. 'I'm not
sure which way you'll go.'

'What do you mean?' I'd ask, surprised.

'You're not really grasping it yet are you? You haven't really got
hold of what it is you are trying to do. I played in your position; I was
a wide man at Liverpool. I think I know what you're going through.'
And, not aware I was 'going through' anything, I'd ask: 'Well, what
exactly are you trying to say Jim?'

'Well, I think you've still got a lot to learn, but I think you'll do it. I
think you can be good, but there are things you are doing at the
moment that aren't right.' And with that, he'd take off into tactics and
the finer points of the game, and after an hour I'd be sitting there wondering: 'What the hell did I do to deserve this?'

After a couple of months, however, my impression of him changed.
As I watched and listened to him more, I slowly began to appreciate
his experience in the game, began to like and respect him more. After
a while, it wasn't uncommon for us to share a drink on Saturdays and
get 'deep and philosophical' over chicken chow mein. That was the
thing about Jim. The longer the night drew on, the deeper and more
philosophical he'd get. 'This is what football is all about,' he'd say.
'Listen to me, son. I know. I've been there.' He'd say it, not in a
boastful or pretentious way, but like the wise old man whose only
wish before dying was to impart what he had learnt to his son. He
wasn't a man ever to go overboard in his praise of individuals, so I
really knew I was getting there when one night, after a game at West
Ham, he pulled me over and said: 'Has he [the manager] said anything
much to you?'

'No, what about Jim?'

'Well, about how you are doing... how you are playing.'

'No.'

'Well, I think you are playing really well and I'm surprised he hasn't pulled you and encouraged you to "keep it up", because that's what I would have done.' I thanked him for the compliment. It made me feel really good. We might have ended up in Happy Talk that night... I'm not sure.

Now, Jimmy still lived in Brighton, and it didn't make sense for him to drive home and then have to come back for the meeting next day. So, with Jackie up in London, I asked him to come back and stay with me for the night. We opened another beer, began to talk. Jimmy liked to get inside your head.

eeeaaarrryoo...

Tired... so tired... head so heavy on the pillow... that sound, a yelp, familiar, coming from somewhere downstairs. Jimmy.... *Chaz*, our dog. 'Oh, no, he's got Chaz. He has him on the couch. He's telling him how to lead his life.* I should go down; I should rescue Chaz, but then he'll corner me again.' Tired, so tired. Blissfully, I drift to sleep. *'Ahhh.'* There's someone in the bed with me. *'Ahhh*. It's Jimmy. He's got his fingers around my throat... he's throttling the life out of me.

I scream: 'Jimmy for fuck's sake!'

He laughs: 'I love you, I love you deeply!'

After a brief and comical struggle he leaves the room.

eeeearrryooo....

That sound. Chaz is yelping again. I really should go down. I jump out of bed, cross the bedroom floor... and twist the key in the lock. 'Sorry Chaz.'

PART 2:

LONG NIGHTS IN ORLANDO... MORE ABOUT JIM

Midnight. On the night after the defeat by Holland, my mind returns to Jim. We've been sitting around the dinner table getting deep and philosophical – myself, Kev (Kevin Moran), Cass (Tony Cascarino) and Aldo (John Aldridge). Coffee follows dessert. A beer leads to another. We look back. We look forward. The talk is football. The end of this team... the future of the next... of life itself. 'Life is life,' Jimmy used to say. Funny, but I am reminded more and more of him and the things he used to say as the night wears on.

01:00 We sip, we reminisce – it seems only yesterday that we were in Cagliari, striding out to play England in our first World Cup game. Sheeds (Kevin Sheedy) and Chris (Morris) were with us then; big Mick (McCarthy) was captain. It's funny, but I've watched Mick a lot these past few days, analysed the chemistry between him and the team – accepted, always, as 'one of the lads' – there was something odd about it. Deep down, it wasn't the same. And it got me thinking – in four years' time, when I stand where Mick stands now, will it be the same for me? Probably.

02:00 Another beer, another story. Gary Kelly sits at a table nearby. Reflecting on his performances and meteoric rise to fame, I am reminded of the pop group who go straight to number one with their first hit single – incredible! When I was nineteen, I was playing amateur with Welling United and here he is, a great season in the Premier League and a World Cup campaign already under his belt. Not that I would want to swap places. Nodding in his direction, I say to Kevin: 'I don't envy him.'

'What do you mean you don't envy him?'

'Well, you're still playing at thirty-eight, but he's got nineteen years before he reaches that stage, sixteen before he is entitled to his [football] pension. I'll be fifty then, you'll be nearly sixty, and Gary Kelly might still be running out to play another World Cup. How on earth is he going to keep doing it?'

'Ah,' says Kev, 'he will, of course he will. You can't wish your life away like that.'

'No, but think about it again,' I insist. 'In three years time he'll be twenty-two – experienced, with a lot of caps. You were only starting at that age – everything was fresh, new to you – that has to make it difficult for him.'

As the debate continues, I consider our respective careers and wonder if the game hasn't been more of a struggle for me. Kevin started off at Manchester United, established himself in the first team and before long was rewarded with success. I, on the other hand, spent four years struggling at Southampton, two at Norwich with relative success – although we never won anything the team performed well – and from there moved to Chelsea and another three seasons of drought. Although I was finally rewarded at Villa with a League Cup winner's medal last March, has the length of the road I have travelled coloured my impressions of the game? Perhaps.

03:00 This is too deep, much too deep. I'm beginning to sound like Jimmy now. As I head off to bed, the realisation that our World Cup has ended again hits home. For five weeks we've been like rock stars on the road, but now the corridors are empty, the party has moved on with the Dutch to Dallas. We are rock stars no more. I slip the card into the slot of 811 – this room that had become my home. There will be no going training in the morning, no early-morning breakfast call. Our World Cup is over. All that is left to remind me it was real are the four soiled shirts – Italian, Mexican, Norwegian and Dutch – that lie discarded on the floor.

Outside it's America

Orlando
(June 6 to June 12)

DAY 1

MONDAY JUNE 6:

TAKE-OFF: WHAT THE PAPERS SAY

Mick Byrne raps on the door just after nine. The World Cup starts here. In a little over an hour, I will kiss my wife goodbye and begin the first leg of a journey that will take me to an event I will look back on for the rest of my life. Not, mind you, that I'm looking forward to it with much enthusiasm: yesterday at Lansdowne Road, in our last warm-up game before the going gets seriously tough, a Czechoslovak wished me luck with an elbow in the face and this morning I most definitely don't like Mondays. My nose, bulbous and throbbing, feels the size of the Eiffel Tower and I'd cover my head with a paper bag if I thought I could find one big enough. Things, as they say, can only get better....

Despite the defeat of yesterday, the headlines in the papers are kind: 'A shock defeat but let's look forward to America' is the common theme, and for once I am pleased to comply. In fairness, Czechoslovakia were a good team, but our minds have been elsewhere all week and our preparation wasn't right. (We were modelling suits for a team photograph a couple of hours before the game.) Over the next twelve days, however, things will be different. The send-off at the airport is great, but it feels good to step on the plane. Away from the hype it will be easier to focus on the task ahead and the first big game.

One of the highlights of my thirteenth year, as I was growing up in South London, was a trophy I won with my team, St Thomas More. I remember feeling pretty pleased with myself, not only because we had won and I was captain, but because the medals and trophy were always presented by a leading professional. This morning, the man who had presented me with the trophy all those years ago was sitting on our flight to New York. I hadn't noticed him in the airport terminal: detained by a reception and a final salute to the fans, we were last to board the plane and it wasn't until we were making our way through the rows of seated passengers that one of the lads highlighted his presence. 'There's Dunphy,' he said. And sure enough, there he was. 'My goodness, hasn't he changed!'

For Dunphy, read Eamon Dunphy; yesterday (or the day before) a professional footballer with Millwall; today, one of the most controversial commentators on the game. Moving on to my seat, I couldn't help but be struck by how intimidated we seemed by his presence. I'm not sure who it was who actually told me he was aboard, but there seemed a genuine hint of fear in his tone. It wasn't just a flat, matter-of-fact statement. It was more as if this small man with the curls and wrinkled face was some kind of ogre, although I've never looked on him like that. While I don't bother much with newspapers or with what sportswriters have to say, I must admit that I occasionally look for Dunphy on the weekend of a game. A good writer and an undoubtedly intelligent man, he has written some stuff over the years that has been absolutely spot on, and I would almost say I was a fan if it wasn't for those times when he has been so outrageously over the top that he has angered me to the point of swearing.

His criticism of Mick McCarthy before the last World Cup was a notable example. Mick, it's true, mightn't have been the most graceful Irish player ever to walk out at Lansdowne Road, but then Jack wasn't looking for a 'Swan Lake' centre half. What he did have, with his massive heart and great balls, was the ability to lead. But Dunphy went for him with a venom that I could never understand. I mean, there's criticising people and there's sticking the knife in – and some of the things he wrote about Mick bordered on the vindictive. His articles of recent times have mellowed somewhat. After the frenzied peak of four years ago, when he was throwing pens around the TV studio in disgust and ashamed to be Irish, he doesn't seem to be pointing the finger quite as much these days. But then, with the results we've being having these past two years, that would be difficult, wouldn't it? How can you criticise success and stay credible? Still, no doubt his presence will make for an interesting few weeks.

Another newspaper I look for when I'm in Dublin before a game is the *Irish Times*, with Mark Lawrenson's column. Mark gives opinions – and players are always interested in the opinions of those who once played the game. Not, mind you, that I would always agree with him either. And as for some of the converted analysts currently doing the rounds on TV – they never cease to amaze. I mean, having played the game you would imagine at least that they (the TV analysts) could   distinguish between a good player and an average player, a class player and a hard-working player. But then the game gets so much easier once you don a shirt and tie. On the few occasions when I've done it myself, I've tried to be balanced and fair. I'd always try to be sympathetic and say, 'Well, that sort of thing can happen to anyone,' when a player's error leads to a goal, (a) because it can and (b) because I know what it feels like when you make a slip like that. Perhaps I'll change my tune once I've stepped outside the game.... I hope not.

If these reflections on players and press seem strange on the opening day, then they have been brought on not only by Eamon Dunphy's unexpected presence on the plane but by some comments by our team-mate Dave O'Leary in yesterday's *News of the World*. Now, before setting off into very delicate territory, let me first say that in my five years of involvement with the Irish team, I have never known Dave O'Leary speak unkindly of anyone. Dave is a smashing fellow and an absolute gent and has always been brilliant to me. Which is why yesterday's article and something else which happened recently struck me as a little strange. On the night that England played Norway in a friendly international two weeks ago, our squad were together at the Nuremore hotel. We sat down to watch the match (we play Norway in three weeks' time, remember) and were interested that Dave had been invited on to the panel as one of the analysts. When it was over and the panellists had finished giving their views on the 'new-look' England, Dave was asked: 'What about Ireland?'

'Well, I don't really know,' he replied. 'I haven't heard from Jack, haven't heard much at all. I don't even hear from the physio these days.' Now, for the benefit of the ill-informed, it must be explained that our physio, Mick Byrne, is more, much more, than the strains and knocks repairman of the team. He is its heart and soul, a communal mother who is never off the phone. So I knew, watching, that Mick would feel quite hurt by this, for he has known Dave and Dave's parents for years. In fairness to Dave, it may be he didn't mean it to sound the way that it came out, but....

Yesterday's piece in the *News of the World* has also left me scratching my head. In an article with Paul McCarthy, spread across two pages, Dave was asked for his 'verdict' on each of our players. A couple, including my own, were fine:

Phil Babb: 'Confidence on legs. The lad has done superbly for Coventry this season. Now I think he could do with a big move. Great pace, great faith in his ability, I'm sure he'll be at the heart of Jack's defence.'

Denis Irwin: 'I've known players to faint when Denis opens his mouth in the dressing-room. The quietest fella you could meet, but so consistent – the lads have opened a book on when his first bad game will be.'

Andy Townsend: 'Biggest mickey-taker in the squad. Great pals with Tony Cascarino, though you'd never guess it the way Andy rips him apart. Jack idolises him.'

But some of the others:

Alan Kernaghan: 'He'd be the first to admit he's had a nightmare season. He's lost his pace, his confidence and his touch. Now Manchester City have put him on the list. But Jack's faith keeps him in the squad. That will lift Alan.'

Kevin Moran: 'Spain exposed his lack of pace and I think he'll admit he doesn't get the trip in the Premiership; but a great servant. If Ireland have to defend for their lives on the edge of their box, there's no better man.'

Ray Houghton: 'Little Hitler or Mister Moan – Ray's always shouting his mouth off and whingeing about something. A great double act with John Aldridge – they're like Siamese twins when they're away. Hasn't been on top form for Villa this season but he's still likely to start.'

David Kelly: 'He's one player who *will* come home bronzed. Loves his clothes, is fanatical about his hair and is a walking suntan. The squad's Mister Cool.'

John Aldridge: 'Typical Scouser – always has something to say even if it doesn't make too much sense. Has the thankless task of running his backside off on his own in the heat but will never moan about it. Hasn't got the goals he would like this season, but always likely to pop up with a vital one.'

Ronnie Whelan: 'Perhaps we've seen the last days of Ronnie. Hasn't been a regular for quite a while, but his experience will be vital if it comes to a crunch match.'

After reading the article, some of the lads were justifiably annoyed, because, after all, if it wasn't for his injury Dave would probably be here with us now. Now again, in fairness, this *is* the *News of the World* and I'm sure he's just the victim of a tabloid sting. It happens; I've been stung once or twice myself.

⚽   ⚽   ⚽

During my second season at Chelsea, on the eve of an FA Cup tie against Everton – mid-table in the League and out of the League Cup, our only shot at glory for the year – I was asked by the manager, Ian Porterfield, to have a word with the press. The interview consisted of most of the usual questions, but then towards the end I was asked: 'Where will it leave you, if tomorrow Chelsea are knocked out?'

So I answered: 'Well, like the rest of the lads, I'll be absolutely choked if we get beat.'

Obviously not quite what they were looking for, so they tried again: 'But where will it leave you and your career with Chelsea?'

'Well, I've still got three years of my contract to run and I'm sure we can achieve something between now and then.'

Again, I wasn't piping to their tune: 'Will it not tempt you to think that your future lies elsewhere?' they asked.

'No,' I replied. So anyway, the following morning, a couple of hours before the game, I picked up the paper and the headline read: 'WIN OR I QUIT.' But I never said that.

My second, and most painful, lesson from the tabloids happened at the end of the same year. We were all sitting round after training one day, discussing our nominations for the PFA (Players' player of the year) awards when, for a bit of a laugh, I suggested we nominate a team of the most ugly as well. This met with a great response, and as the boys started shouting out names, I began jotting them down; Kev was in there and Peter Beardsley. Now there was nothing nasty intended, and anyway none of this would escape beyond the dressing-room wall – it was just a joke among ourselves. So you can imagine my surprise a few days later when, just as I arrived for training, Cass (Tony Cascarino) burst out laughing.

'Brilliant article, Andy. I pissed myself laughing all the way in.'

(Surprised.) 'What are you talking about?'

'Your ugly team. It's in the *Sun*. Brilliant, mate.'

'Whaaat! You must be joking!'

'No, look,' and he handed me a copy.

Now at this stage I must point out that two days earlier 'the team' had found its way into the official supporters' paper, and while this had made me uncomfortable, it was nothing to how I felt when I saw it in the *Sun*, where not only had they printed photographs of those 'selected' but had captioned them for effect with headings like 'UGHHH!' Furious, I rang the journalist whose name was attached to the story and demanded a retraction. This wasn't just any 'Ugly 11' after all, it was 'Andy Townsend's Ugly 11' and what had started as a (very) private joke was now doing the rounds in four million homes in Britain. More embarrassed than at any other time in my life, I made a desperate attempt to repair the damage and explained and apologised to those who had been maligned. Which is what puzzles me about Dave. If what he said *was* misinterpreted, then he knew how to reach us yesterday; could have phoned the hotel this morning. But so far we haven't heard from him and Ray and Kev and some of the others he was harsh on are still wondering whether they should take what they read as his word.

⚽   ⚽   ⚽

The journey to Orlando was a tale of contrasting flights. The first, an Aer Lingus flight from Dublin to New York, was a joy: seven hours of being spoiled rotten on an A310 – one of the most modern aircraft in the sky. The second, a TWA flight from New York, was a rather less pleasant experience: a two-hour hop on a B727 that looked like it had been dragged straight from a breakers' yard. Now, while I don't mind flying, when you are 30,000 feet high in a thing with multi-coloured seats and a body that looks like someone has been throwing stones at it, it's hard not to feel a touch at risk. 'Crikey! What was that bang? Er... can I have another beer please?'

Twelve hours after leaving Dublin, it was nice to touch down at last on Orlando's soil. It was cloudy and overcast, and the hot, humid air immediately taxed the breath as we stepped off the plane. A coach, waiting on the Tarmac, transported us straight to our hotel, where we have exclusive access to the eighth floor. It seems okay.

DAY 2

TUESDAY JUNE 7:

OUTSIDE IT'S AMERICA

Orlando is a funny sort of place. I've been here twice before on holiday. Loved it the first time: Wet N'Wild, Seaworld, Disney; was less enthusiastic the second: Wet N'Wild, Seaworld, Disney. And after my first day in the place third time around, I am now of the definite opinion that I couldn't live in a place surrounded by theme parks. But it's more than just Mickey Mouse; take, for example, the TV here. At home, when I flick through the channels I am often of the opinion that there is nothing on the four worth a look. But here, there are twenty channels with even less to offer: *Jeopardy*, *Family Fortunes*, game show after game show. And then there's the evening news – CNN, ABC, NBC – where 'eyewitness' is a catch-phrase and the news is not only always bad, but five times worse than at home. And then there's the baseball (can't stand it) and the.... No, my mind is made up. Once this World Cup is out of the way, Orlando will have to wait a while before it sees my money again.

The thing is that attitudes, outlook and the whole pace of life are different here, so different that although we've just popped across from the other side of the Atlantic, we might easily have beamed down from Mars. Take the people and their attitude to football – sorry, soccer. In a survey in one of the papers this morning, I read that 60 per cent of Americans didn't know that the World Cup was being held in their country! Can you believe that?

Basically, what we are dealing with here are two alien cultures. The press conference that followed our training session this morning was a notable example. An American reporter asked: 'Andy, could I just ask you what your 'deee-fensive' tactics are going to be?'

'You what mate?'

'Could you explain what Ireland's defensive tactics are going to be?'

'Er, not to let any goals in.'

(Shocked) 'Is that it?'

'Yeah, that's it.'

So then he asked: 'Well what about *off*ence. What are your plans offensively?'

'Well, we wanna score, mate. Forgive me, but in soccer, when you don't let none in and you score a goal or two you're doing just fine. There might be some tactics along the way, but I'm sorry, that's about the best way I can sum it up.'

But he was still looking at me as if I had two heads, which is worrying when you consider that next week this is a guy who is going to be reporting on the game. Like I say, football, as we know it, is alien here. You see, the thing about sport and the great American youth is, if he's tall, he will play basketball. If he's tall and well-built he'll play American football. If he's fast he'll do athletics. If he is all of the above and intelligent, he'll play golf. And if he is none of the above, he'll end up playing baseball. (Sorry baseball fans, but I really don't appreciate your sport.)

Another problem of selling soccer to the masses is marketing. For the last hour, I've been sitting watching the New York Knicks play the Houston Rockets in the opening game of the NBA finals, bombarded with 'time-outs' and 'quarters' and 'facts' or 'stats' as they are known here. How many times John Stark touched the ball, what percentage of Hakeem Olajuwon's shots have been on target – it is easy to be drawn by the excitement of it all and, watching, it suddenly dawned on me how slow and laid back our game must seem in comparison. Everything about this seems designed to keep you on the edge of your seat, even the players – such characters, such mountains of men – it's as if they've all been hand-picked for the roles. Now maybe, when you've been reared on so much razzmatazz, the prospect of watching ninety minutes of a scoreless drawn soccer match isn't all that appealing. I don't know. It should be interesting to see how it will go.

Home, for the next ten days, is room 811 of the North Orlando Hilton. A single room with a double bed, where the in-house comforts consist of a TV, mini-bar and an air-conditioning system that sounds like it's being powered by a Ferrari V12. It doesn't, I imagine, differ greatly from room 811 of the Salt Lake City Hilton or the South Seattle Hilton. See one and you've seen them all.

This morning begins in the traditional way – Mick (Byrne) rapping on the door, with me ignoring his pleas to leave the bed as I try to work out what kind of day it is beyond the small gap in the curtains. Too dark to be sunny. I'm right about the cloud but not the rain. Charlie

(O'Leary), has my kit piled up outside the door when eventually I find the motivation to stir, but before I can pull a sock on, I am dragged stark naked by the doctor to the weighing scales and am weighed.

After breakfast, it's time to go to work. The training ground is a 25-minute drive from the hotel. Facilities are good – fully equipped gym, decent showers and two pitches with playing surfaces that are truly excellent. Before the session in the rain kicks off, Jack gathers us round under the shelter of a small marquee and lays down some ground-rules for the duration of our stay.

'Right,' he says. 'One: From now on, everyone is going to do as they are told.

'Two: This is the United States of America, a place where crime and murder occur almost as frequently as these thunderstorms we've been having [it has been raining since we touched down]. Don't go anywhere unless people know (a) where you are going and (b) who you are with. No one goes outside the hotel without my permission or one of the staff's permission.

'Three: We are here to do a job, not mess about. You don't drink tap water. You eat only what is served up to you at mealtimes. If you need anything, ask and you shall receive.

'Four: If anyone is taking any medication at all – hay fever pills, tablets, whatever – these must be noted and approved by the doctor.'

The work-out, when it starts, is difficult enough. The temperature, despite the rain, is warm and clammy, and what would normally have been a steady session to get everyone's heart and lungs going is made more difficult by Jack's insistence that we wear these heavy training tops to make us sweat. I asked if I could take mine off. When you are running around, it's not easy to get the quality into your work when you are weighed down by a top so wet it weighs three or four pounds. But Jack didn't want to know – and when Jack doesn't want to know, it doesn't help to argue. You just get on with it.

The opening session over, we shower and are weighed again and have each lost a couple of pounds. After the press conference and lunch, there is a second session where we work for a further hour and twenty minutes – shooting, crossing, ball-work – then it's back on the bus for the return to the hotel. When I return to my room, the small red light on my telephone is flashing. I contact the receptionist who tells me that an Una McNelis has called and will call back. The name means nothing to me.

✲　　✲　　✲

Explaining Una McNelis: Two colours Browne

A tanned American lady from Daytona Beach, Florida, invites me to a table in the lobby of the Hilton Hotel. She opens a book called *Tracing Your Ancestry* by F. Wilbur Helmbold, points out her name – Una McNelis – and place of birth – New York – then takes me branch by branch through her family tree. She's one of three girls whose father, Bernard McNelis, was born in Ardara, Co. Donegal while her mother, Noreen Browne came from Castleisland, Co. Kerry. Her (maternal) grandfather Jackie was also from Castleisland, as was her great-grandfather John – the root that brings her to the Irish team hotel today. John Browne, you see, happens to be my great-grandfather as well. A tailor by day and Irish Republican Brotherhood member by night (he was lucky to escape on the night Roger Casement was arrested off Bannow Strand), he lived with his wife Mary in a small house in Barrack Street, Castleisland. On January 12, 1896, Mary gave birth to a baby girl – Bridgid.

Bridgid Browne was eighteen, at the time of the Easter Rising. She travelled to Dublin from her native Castleisland to find work and was taken on as a housemaid by a doctor in Rathmines. After four years in the capital, she met and began 'walking out' with a soldier in the British army. Cecil George Townsend seemed a decent man. They married in a church in Rathmines in 1924, then left for England to begin their new life together at Cecil's parents' home in Swindon. When they arrived, however, there were problems. Cecil's mother, of staunch Church of England stock, refused to let them sleep together until she was assured they had been 'properly' married. So they married again, this time at the local register office, where Bridgid, who had always been called 'Bridggy' in Ireland and hated it, changed her Christian name to Beatrice. (A minor detail that 65 years on would cause Andy, her grandson, untold grief – but more of that later.)

They settled down to married life and started a family. Cecil got a job with the Great Western Railway, while Beatrice looked after Kenneth, their new-born son. Kenneth died at the age of three, but four other children would grow up strong and healthy. A set of twins, Burt and Roy was followed by another boy, Don, and then a girl, Glenys. For fifteen years, they lived a settled and normal life until the war broke out in 1939 and Cecil went back to the army. Beatrice watched as her husband walked off to war; her life would never be the same again.

Don, my father, remembers a pretty good childhood for his first nine years. Summers were religiously spent in Ireland. School term over, they would take the train to Fishguard, the boat to Rosslare, another train via Mallow to Killarney and then the branch line to Castleisland. Home for the summer was his grandparents' old tin-roofed house in Barrack Street, where his uncle Jackie taught him songs like 'Tour ra loo ra loo' and his mother taught him his prayers in Irish: '*In anim an athair, agus an mhic....* ' Swindon, too, was a fun place to grow tall. His dad, who was a big football fan, used throw them a tennis ball and watch them chase it on the streets – not because he knew it would make them better players, but because he couldn't afford the real thing.

Then the war broke out and his dad went away. He returned once or twice on leave during the first three years... and then nothing except for the letter that depressed his mum and made her burst into tears. Although it was never explained to him, slowly he began to understand he had seen the last of his Dad. It didn't greatly trouble him at the time; twelve is a funny age for boys. He had his mum, his brothers, his mates on the street. He didn't really need a dad.

Don was fifteen years old when the war ended; he got a job at the rail-yard and began to take his football more seriously – not that you could call the Sunday kick-about at the recreation ground serious. Glassy eyed and a little unsteady on their feet, the opposition would drift out of the pub in the afternoon and, tucking his trouser-legs into his socks, Don would join his mates and make them sweat for the afternoon. It was a neighbour, 'Niggy' Laverne, who recommended him to Charlton Athletic. They watched him in a couple of games and, suitably impressed agreed to sign him as a professional on the completion of his two years' national service in 1950.

Football, it must be remembered, was a very different game then. Charlton, FA Cup winners three years earlier, were one of the biggest clubs in England, with home attendances regularly topping 70,000, and more than fifty players on their books. There were no guarantees that my father, twenty years old when he made the trip to London, was going to be good enough. He settled in digs near the ground, was paid a wage of seven pounds a week and played with the reserves for the first half of the season, until one morning at training a spate of injuries unexpectedly opened the door. 'I want to see you play this week son,' his manager, Jimmy Seed announced. 'How do you feel about playing with the first team?' Shy and reticent by nature, my dad suggested modestly that he wasn't sure he was ready. He often laughs about that now. 'Blessed are the meek, for they shall get trampled on.' It was four years before they offered him a chance again. That was 1954. He remembers his debut – all footballers do. He was selected at right back for an away game at Leicester and they won 2–1. His wages went up a fiver to twelve pounds a week after that. And there was also the four pound bonus for winning the game. He settled into his new life, was switched from right back to left back, and over the next eight years made the position his own.

A strange thing happened at an away game at Hull one Saturday. He was just about to leave the hotel with the rest of the team for the ground, when he was given a message that there was someone asking for him downstairs. When he went down, a man wrapped in coat and cap stepped forward: 'Hello, son, I'm your Dad.' Not that my father needed reminding; he knew who he was, for twenty years had aged but not altered his features. They sat down. Exchanged small talk. And when it was time to leave for the ground, my grandfather was brought on to the coach and given a ticket to the game. They met again when it was over. After briefly explaining he was living on his own, my grandfather switched back to the game, where they both seemed more comfortable. Although it seems an obvious thing to do, my father never asked why. How, after all, could Cecil possibly explain? He had walked out on his wife and children, had abandoned both his parents – had never returned for their funeral or placed a flower on their grave. They knew the reason; they knew about the other woman. But how could he explain?

When it was time for my father to leave, they agreed that they should both keep in touch, and perhaps they might have if Beatrice hadn't been so upset when she learned of the 'visit'. As a result, my father never saw him again. Beatrice died in 1979. Cecil did not came to the funeral. Ten years later, when my dad went looking for her death certificate, to establish my credentials for playing for Ireland, he came across another Townsend in the book – his father. He had died, three years earlier, in Hull in 1986. The contrast in reactions when my father informed his brothers was interesting. Although obviously saddened, my father felt very little. But Roy, whose memories of Cecil were a good deal stronger, was moved to tears.

All things considered, 1954 was a significant year for Don Townsend. A regular on the first team, he began cutting some ice with a girl called

Thelma Leaver, whose garden backed onto the digs where he was staying at the time. Thelma gets quite animated when you quiz her about him then. All the things she admired in him on their first date to the pictures – his soft Wiltshire accent, his placidness, his dry humour, the huge streak of Irishness he inherited from his mother – drive her 'potty' now. My mother, a died-in-the-wool Londoner with the Londoner's razor wit, has always had the ability to carve my father up at will. Sometimes we might be sitting having dinner and, responding to some casual reference to bombing during the war, my dad might say: 'Cor, yeah, that wasn't much fun.' But my Mum, who would look at him like he had just grown another head, would instantly shoot him down: 'They weren't dropping bombs in bleedin' Wiltshire!'

Despite the occasional difference of opinion, however, they have seasoned well and although my mother would undoubtedly deny it, the flame that brought them together forty years ago still burns today. They were married in July 1956 and Mike, their first born in 1957, was followed by twins (they run in the family) Kenneth and Karen in 1959. The family should have ended there – three children was to be the quota – but nature has its way. Accidents do happen and four years later in July of '63 they had one, a blue-eyed beauty weighing a magnificent ten pounds. They called him Andy.

DAY 3

WEDNESDAY JUNE 8:

BLACK DAYS, BRIGHT NIGHTS

We've come here for sun. We've come here to acclimatise to the humidity and heat that will play a vital role in our opening games. But it was raining again this morning; absolutely poured down, and though that meant an 'easier' day, I wasn't that pleased when I pulled back the curtains. I was really looking forward to a work-out in the sun. The thing is, with just ten days to go now before our opening game, we need to suffer. We need to know what it will be like to be dying of thirst, to have to struggle to catch a breath. Alas, for the second day running, we were forced to train in the wet. The morning session was a complete disaster – we'd only just run out when we were ordered off the pitch. Lightning was the problem. This is the lightning capital of the world and to play football when it's flashing all around you is to risk frying to a crisp.

The return indoors, however, did have its pluses. After a short work-out in the gym followed by lunch, Eddie McGoldrick gave me the old 'nudge nudge' and showed me how to dial home from this phone he found in an office. I rang Jackie, who's staying with her mother, had a quick word with Daniel 'Have you been a good boy?' and a quick word with Kelly 'Have you been a good girl' and then ran out of things to say. It's not that I was worried about the bill, you understand. It's just, well, I'm not really the type for 'I love yous' down the line. Once I know everything is okay, I'm gone.

In the afternoon, as the word spread about the phone and the boys began to bicker (as to who was next to use it), the arrival of the sun sent us all back to work. Although it was still not a totally cloudless sky, I managed to shed five pounds, which set me wondering as to how much I will lose when we play Mexico in a fortnight's time. Entertainment this evening was an organised trip to Seaworld, but I couldn't face it. Having visited twice before I feel I'm on first-name terms, with Shamu (the killer whale) at this stage.

'Hello Sham.'

'Oh hello, Andy old son, how are Jackie and the kids?'

When they returned, what was left of the day was killed with a couple of games of Scrabble – me and Cass against the Charltons, Jack and his son John. Jack, although tired, was up to his usual tricks and tried to intimidate us with what we knew was a dodgy word: s-t-o-a-k-e-r.

'What's stoaker?' I asked.

'Stoaker, as in fire,' Jack replied.

'There's no "a" in stoker,' I argued. 'It's s-t-o-k-e-r.'

'It isn't,' he bellowed, adamant as ever. An adjudicator was brought in. Kevin Moran was sitting playing cards at a table nearby. I asked: 'How do you spell stoker Kev?' And of course we were right, so the lads had to drop the 'a'. Then there was another argument over the spelling of 'trek', with team Charlton wanting to add a 'c'. For the second time of the evening it went to adjudication and for the second time the judge ruled in our favour. Cheers Kev. We won easily in the end. Jack was not pleased.

⚽   ⚽   ⚽

Bexleyheath boy

My son, Daniel, knows. I know he knows. When we're out together and a stranger walks up and says, 'Hello Andy, what about...' I can see it in his eyes. The buzz, the kick that gives him. He knows not to ask who they are; understands why people are friendly. His dad, you see, is recognised. He's seen it. He knows.

I was seven years old when I realised my dad was a 'someone'. We were sitting at home one night when he asked me if I wanted to go and see him play. Five years retired, he had been asked to turn out in a Crystal Palace 'old boys' versus 'new boys' testimonial for a former team-mate of his, John Sewell. (Following twelve years at Charlton, he had finished his career after three seasons with Palace in 1965.) I had never seen him play before and, watching from the stands as he struggled to get off his toes, it was no great comfort to me that he was forty years old.

When it was over, I was invited to join him in the players' lounge and was walking around, trying to match the faces to the people I'd seen on the pitch, when I noticed my father with a famous face. Okay, so the players weren't exactly nobodies but this was a *real* famous face. My dad was talking to Brian Moore, the commentator on *The Big*

Match. I couldn't believe it. I mean, from the scrap-books and photo albums at home, I was aware of my father's career and that he had been decent enough in his time, but I had no idea he was this good. This was the voice that used ring in my ears each time I kicked a ball on the street: 'Townsend. Oooh what a goal!' And my dad, he was talking to him, talking to Brian Moore. Nice one, Dad.

The game. It takes you. Transforms you. One minute you're a face without features, the next you're a face people place. The game does that for you; it suckles you, fattens you, brings you money and respect; it takes you and makes you dependent – and then it dumps you. Drops you for someone else. The game is good but the game is cruel.

Dad was thirty-five when the game let him go. He'd seen it coming and had been wondering about what he would do since the move from Charlton in '62. Strange at the end the way you notice things you hadn't noticed before, like the old pros hovering around the honey pot on match days – the pitiful souls who had been dropped but couldn't let go. That wouldn't be him. He'd not be back. His would be a new life. A fresh start. But what? The game had been his life for seventeen years. What could he do?

Some sort of commerce seemed ideal. He bought a shop, a newsagent's in Bexley, and supplemented his income with some coaching on the side. The first two years were hard, and though he stayed away from the Palace, letting go was easier said than done. Life in the shop was so flat, so even. There were none of the massive highs of the game and none of its desperate lows: people paid the same price for the same paper, day after day, week after week, and after three years he decided he had had enough. A brother of my mum's owned a computer punch card business that was thriving and, taking up his offer of a job, they sold the shop and moved to a detached four-bedroom house just up the road.

My earliest childhood memories are of the paper shop in Bexley. When I was four years old, I would stand by the counter with my dad, then race out the door as soon as a customer pulled up and hold open the door of his car. Dad used complain about it. 'They're getting excellent service and only buying a paper,' he'd say. But I didn't mind. I liked chatting, always wanted to know more about the adult world.

Bexleyheath wasn't a bad place to grow up. I was always a 'lad', always one of the boys out on the street, but rarely got into trouble. I had this talent, you see, this knack for spotting danger; the sin after all wasn't in being mischievous but in getting caught. And those who don't have the knack are always getting caught. Take my older brother, Ken, for example: he works hard, he works his nuts off, and yet as hard as he works he'll still get done for a £75 speeding ticket at the silliest time of day. Then, to compound matters, he won't pay it. Seething, he'll sit on it for a while, forget about it and end up paying double. He was like that in school, too; he was often in trouble. But not me. As much as I was always part of the gang – if not at the head of it – I would never race blindly into anything without first stopping to think. At school, while sitting among the mannerly and courteous in the middle of the class, I still retained 'cred' with my mates down the back.

Other memories are of Beatrice, my nan who was living with my Aunt Glenys in the house in Swindon that she had once shared with Cecil. We visited once a month. Dad would pack us into the car for the three-hour journey that today you might make in one. There was no M4 back then, of course, and Dad never drove faster than 40 miles an hour. Swindon in the sixties was different too. I am often reminded of it when I pass through some of the towns and villages in Ireland and see the gates flung wide and the hall doors open. It was a quiet, country town.

Because of my dad's former profession, Nan always treated him as a bit of a celebrity whenever we visited. My mum often tells the story about one day when her drain was blocked. My dad and his brother Roy both walked outside to clear it, but when she saw my Dad rolling up his sleeve she was horrified: 'What are you doing Don? Roy! Get your bloody hand down there.' Apart from her good sense of humour, I remember her most for her accent. Sometimes, she might ask me something and I wouldn't have a clue what she was saying. As I cocked my head quizzically, my Dad would interpret: 'Your nan says.... ' But I was baffled, didn't understand about Ireland or Kerry. I was from Kent – people didn't talk like that around Bexleyheath. Although she occasionally visited at weekends, she didn't like travelling and what with school and playing football at weekends, I didn't see as much of her as I grew toward my teens. She died ten years before my first appearance for Ireland but my dad – who, like the rest of my family, always uses 'we' when talking about Ireland's games – seems to think she would have liked the idea.

St Thomas More and Teviot Rangers were arch rivals in Bexleyheath. I was nine years old and captain of St Thomas More when they met in the '72 Cup final, a game that has remained with me to this day. (*Apology*: If there is one thing that cracks me up about football books in general, it's the way the hero/subject *always* captained his school team as a boy. While it grieves me immensely to follow suit, I do so merely to emphasise that – unlike my predecessors – I did *not* lead by example.)

Dad watched from the sideline. Mum stayed at home. She was funny like that, rarely came to watch us play. The last years of my dad's career had left a mark on her. It wasn't that the game had treated them badly – on the contrary, it had given them a very comfortable life – but to be dumped so brutally at thirty-five, to be cast out into the real world after being cocooned for seventeen years, left a very bitter taste, a taste she hoped her boys would never experience. The problem with football, of course, is that it is such a popular game. We wanted to play, and while she never tried to stop us, she never encouraged us either. She wanted her sons to get good jobs when they left school, not follow in the footsteps of their dad. On the day of the big final, she stayed away.

All through the first half and for most of the second it was dead-locked. Then, with fifteen minutes to go, one of our players went down in their box and the ref pointed to the spot. As captain, and one of the better players on the team, the lads immediately looked to me to take it. And on any other day I would have; on any other day I would have put it down and whacked it without giving it a thought. But this wasn't 'any other day'. This was Teviot Rangers and the final of the Cup. Although the touchline was nigh on deserted, if I had been standing before a packed house at Wembley I couldn't have been more scared. Noticing my reticence, Andy James – the team manager's son – stepped forward. Not the most skilful of our players, he made up in endeavour for what he lacked in skill. Placing the ball, he stood back and surveyed the target. Then, taking a short run, he smacked with his right foot... to the left of the post. He missed. Delighted, Teviot were suddenly full of running and scored the game's only goal five minutes from time. When it was over, I was distraught: 'We had lost... I had bottled it.'

On the way home in the car, my father, intimidated perhaps by my tears, said little. My mother I expected would be more vocal, but instead of 'Don't worry about it, these things happen' when we arrived in the door, there was a full post-mortem on the game. 'You do realise you could have scored the winning goal in the Cup final today,' she chided. 'Why didn't you try? Why didn't you take it? At least if you had missed you'd have had a go. Don't ever be afraid to step forward, there is no shame in trying.' Puzzled at first by her sudden interest in the game, later I would understand that her message was about 'life'.

I stayed with St Thomas More for five seasons in all, then left them to join a friend, Steve Barker, in a team called Interfico. I had played against them before in a couple of Cup competitions, and remembered them most for their huge centre half. He was six foot four, with hairs on his chin, and while the kit was an ample fit for every other boy on the team, Tony Cascarino seemed always to be running round with his shorts up his arse and his manhood hanging out. Running up and down, you would often hear the dads on the touchline giving out about him: 'How old is he? *Fourteen*?' He was always accused of being a 'ringer'. His school, St Joseph's in Orpington, was a fifteen-minute drive from ours in Bexleyheath, but with training two nights a week and a game at weekends, slowly we began to get pally.

It was around this time also that I first met Jackie Evans. I was standing with Steve Barker at the bottom of the stairs in school one day when we noticed her walking down with some of her mates. I nodded to Steve that she seemed a very attractive girl (not my exact words), but was yellow carded immediately for trying to look up her skirt (an outrageous slander totally without foundation). Preferring Steve at first (lousy taste), she went out with him for a couple of years and then he fobbed her off on me. Love at second sight; we've been together ever since.

DAY 4

THURSDAY JUNE 9:

A QUIET DAY AT THE OFFICE

A quiet day at the office; training this morning is a replay of the day before. It is clammy and overcast when we run out, and the session has only just started when we are forced back to the team bus by a huge crack of thunder. The cards are produced and we decide to sit it out, but the rain is heavy, so violently heavy that the bus sinks eight inches into the grass and requires a tow-truck to pull it out. The shower recedes, work resumes and the sun makes a welcome appearance. Before long we are sweating and the morning is thankfully salvaged.

On returning to the club-house for lunch, Jack warns us about sneaking into the office and an arrangement is made for us to pay for our calls. Given the afternoon off, we are driven to the local mall, while the evening's entertainment is pool and a game of darts. Having paid ten dollars to enter, I go out to Cass in the opening round of the pool (which he goes on to win), while at darts, Ray gives us all a lesson on how to pepper the treble 20.

❂   ❂   ❂

Fred, Charlie, the colour of money
I was eighteen years old when I first got the chance to turn pro. The job, the manager informed me, didn't pay as well as the one I had at Greenwich Council (where I was a computer operator), but if I came and practised hard, who knows where it might lead? Tempted, I told him I'd like to sit on it for a night. There's no doubt I had made progress at the game, but good enough to be pro? No, I wasn't sure. And then there was Mum. From the day I had left school – like my brothers and sister before me – she had dragged me around London and done every-thing but the interviews in the quest to find me a job. What would she say? I mean, it would have been bad enough if it was football, but snooker? The misfits' game? No, that would definitely blow her top – and yet, maybe I *was* good enough. With more than fifteen centuries

under my belt, breaks of seventy and eighty were bread and butter to me now. Maybe I could hack it at this game.

From the moment I stepped through the door of Fred Abrams' Snooker Hall in Bexleyheath I was smitten. Snooker was a different game then; we're talking late seventies here, the *Pot Black* days when Ray Reardon ruled and Steve Davis was still singing cabaret in Vegas – or was that Sammy? The halls were different, too – dimly lit, sparsely furnished and covered in a thick choking fog of smouldering cigarettes. There were no plush carpets, velvet walls, fancy lanterns or soft pianos tinkling away in the background. No, they were raw and rough and ready, the classic mis-spent youth. At Fred's, the only background music was the clatter of breaking balls; here, you wiped your feet on the way out.

I was fifteen when my dad took me around. He liked the odd frame of snooker. We used to play on a small table at home but it was nothing compared to this. These were real tables, real games, and I loved it – not just the game but the whole ambience. All of human life was here, a place rich in characters who smoked and drank too much and loved their neighbours – sometimes in the back of parked cars. Sitting and listening to adult tales from the adult world was an education in itself. Tired of knocking on doors and running way, I found it much more interesting being a boy amongst men than a boy amongst boys.

But if it was fun, then it was also dangerous. There was a code of conduct, an etiquette that was unwritten but always obeyed. When you were on a roll and playing well, for example, you couldn't stampede blindly around the table. You had to walk, be careful. With the tables just feet apart, the last thing you wanted to do was nudge a plasterer whose week's wages were riding on the frame alongside: 'Oi, if you don't watch where you're going, I'll throw you down the stairs.' But the rawness, the scent of danger – I loved it. Within weeks, I was on first-name terms with the proprietor and the only kid allowed in with a school uniform on. The teachers used to flip about the stench of cigarettes from my clothes (I'd nip down for a quick frame during break). My mother too. After a while I left a spare set at the club.

Financing my new habit was another early problem. It was a penny a minute to play and there was also the matter of the stake, the wager on the side. Whenever I was overdrawn with Mum, my brother Kenny would help me out, or I would dip into the tin he kept stashed in his room. There was one morning in particular when I was very nearly caught out. Mike, my eldest brother, was the target: he used to stuff his money in a jacket he kept hanging in his wardrobe. The curtains were drawn when I entered. Dipping into his pocket, I hoped for a couple of 50p coins, but there was no loose change – just a note. Thinking it was a pound, I was about to turn and run with it when I heard this groan. Mike! He was asleep in the bed. 'Shit,' I thought. 'He's going to kill me.' Heart pounding, I sprinted out the door and was at the bus stop before I glanced at what I had lifted in my hand – a fiver! 'Oh God, he'll definitely miss that.' Motivated like never before to play well so I could return it, I swore I would never dip into his pocket again.

Although it didn't take me long before I could play, there were days like in everything else, when I just wasn't on form. One night in particular stands out, when I was up against a guy that I could always get the better of. This time he didn't just beat me, he wiped the floor with me and being young and hot headed, I was so annoyed that I hammered the butt of my cue on the floor. Now today, what with the carpets and all, I would probably have got away with it, but on Fred's old stone floor, my cue completely shattered.

Charlie Wise, a plasterer who was a regular at the club, offered me the use of his cue until I had sorted another one out. Now snooker cues are funny old things. Play a lot with the right one and you'll never play with anything else. As soon as I picked up Charlie's cue, it felt perfect; like an extension to my arm. That left me with a bit of a problem, because when I offered Charlie some money for it, he refused point blank to sell. Now Charlie was the world's worst gambler and one night, after he had lost everything but his trousers, I offered him a tenner for it. 'No, no,' he insisted at first, 'I'm not parting with that.' But then he cracked and handed it over and we set up the balls for a frame. Three frames later I had won my tenner back. He was choked. 'Never mind,' I offered, 'you can borrow it [the cue] when I'm not here.'

I liked Charlie. Did a lot of my growing up with guys like him. Like the time he introduced me to The Golden Nugget in Shaftesbury Avenue. Sixteen years old, I knew my taste in clothes (jeans and leather jackets) would never get me past the door of a fashionable London casino, but after a quick detour for something that would from Ken ('You're going *where*? Mum will kill you if she finds out!'), we arranged to meet at Charlie's girlfriend's flat. He was standing outside when I arrived. They had an arrangement where he handed her half his wages each week to stop him blowing it down at the club. But she wasn't home from work so, bunging the money into an envelope, he shoved it in the letter box and we headed off.

Once at the Casino, we had to be prudent with our money, twenty-five quid (Charlie's twenty and my fiver) didn't buy a lot of chips. Watching for a while before taking the plunge, we noticed a Chinese gent gambling seriously at a table. Now when I say seriously, I mean it, because as soon as the croupier would say 'Place your bets', he'd place a mountain of chips each time. And lose. He would lose it every time. After fifteen minutes of the most incredibly rotten luck, he suddenly cracked. Jumping up from the table in a rage, with a swipe of his fist he sent his chips crashing to the floor. As we were all standing there, looking at him, a couple of the staff rushed to his side to help him gather them up. But about eight of them landed half an inch from my foot and with a swift step to the right, I had them covered. The next minute was unbearably tense. Watching as the Chinese marched off, I couldn't believe it. I'd done it. There was 150 quid sitting under my right foot. But then, just as I was about to bend down, I felt this tap on my shoulder. 'Excuse me, son, you do realise that Mr Ying is the only one who can use those chips don't you?'

Playing dumb, I said: 'I'm sorry?'

'Those chips, the ones under your foot. You do realise they're no good to you?'

'Oh Christ. Yeah. Sorry mate.'

The night, when we started, proved just as unlucky for us and by the end we barely had enough for a taxi to Bexleyheath. It was well after midnight when we got back, but Charlie wasn't finished; he had a plan to re-coup our losses. Racing round to his girlfriend's flat with a coat-hanger, he remembered the cash deposit he had made earlier in the evening: 'Come on, Andy, I can feel it. Our luck is just about to turn'

My first century was a milestone. For months I had been there or thereabouts, shooting breaks of eighty and ninety without ever making the ton. And then, one Sunday night, in what I can only describe as the worst possible circumstances, I did it. We were playing on one of the two decent tables out the back. From the break, the balls dropped nicely... 75... 82... and I felt sure I was about to crack it, when it suddenly dawned on me that I hadn't got a witness. The table alongside was empty. My mates were playing out front. The only person in the whole world who could verify my achievement, my first ever break of 105, was the one I was playing against – my dad. Fooling myself that he just might be enough, I raced out front to break the news.

'Lads, I did it! I'm delighted with myself, just put away 105!'

'Yeah? Great, who against?'

'I'm in there, playing me dad.'

'Oh right, good one. I bet you did as well.'

'No, straight up, I did. Dad! Come 'ere a minute.'

Dad being Dad, it wasn't in his nature to start swearing blind about what he had witnessed, and in that typically laid back way of his, he bleated out a timid, 'Oh, I think he did, you know.' Of all the luck!

The early eighties spelt boom-time. Steve Davis was world champion, Hurricane Higgins a household name and you couldn't switch on your TV but there was snooker on the screen. When the game took off I was eighteen years old and working the afternoon shift at Greenwich Council, playing most of my weekday snooker in the morning. (Unless of course I was down a few quid, when the dreaded phone call for 'extra time' would have to be made. Terrified my boss would hear the balls clattering in the background, I'd bury the receiver in my ear and mouth: 'Eh hi, this is Andy. I'm not feeling so well today. I'm not sure I'll be able to come in.') Mum used wake me regularly at nine and I'd be down to Fred's by ten, where the queue would be out the door and down the stairs waiting for it to open. The surge in the game's popularity meant that tables were harder to come by – all it took was half a grey cloud and the place would be heaving with labourers from the building sites. Not that the race to secure a table ever bothered me. Slipping in through the fire escape at the back, I'd have my balls polished and set up on the best table in the house before the doors opened and my first 'customer' arrived. That's what we used call them – the builders and plasterers we'd fleece – our 'customers', because although the game was fun it was also business. I knew the colour of money, wasn't interested in playing wallies for buttons any more. Hustling, though, was a dangerous game, an addiction in itself. There was one morning I went in with fifteen quid in my pocket and was down two hundred by two o'clock. Now, logically, I should have been more than happy to get out at that stage. But the hustler, the gambler, doesn't think along logical lines. He wants to turn it around, win it back. And sometimes I did. But there were other times....

I remember coming straight from work one night with a month's salary in my pocket – a whole month's salary – and I lost it all. Suddenly, the alarm that had always warned me of danger was ringing: 'Be careful Andy. This is dangerous. That's a month's hard-earned salary you've just blown there. Persist with this obsession and you could very easily burn.' It was around this time when Fred made me the offer. 'I can't pay you what you are getting in work, but if you pack up your football and come and play and practise hard, I'll enter you in all of the competitions, you can have as much free time on whatever table you like and I'll get all of the best players in the area to play you. Why not give it a crack?'

I thought about it. I was good, the best in the club. But could I cut it as a pro? No, I couldn't. Mum's reaction was a factor. So was the enjoyment I was getting from togging out on Sundays for Welling United. Ultimately, though, it was the disgust I felt walking home the night I blew my wages that swung it. Because you can't do that. You can't worry about the money riding on the frame. Snooker is a game where the going only really gets tough when the stakes get high. Once you start to look down, you start missing the ball.

In the two years that followed the decline in my interest in snooker, my life began to take shape. Promoted at work, I bought a car and left Welling United for Weymouth, where my weekly appearance for the part-timers was netting a tidy £120 a week. My contract with Jackie was also up for review. After five years of what had been a lengthy and loving partnership (when I wasn't playing snooker), we decided to end it and get married. In the autumn of '84, we took out a mortgage on a house in Bexleyheath and set a date for the execution for May of the following year. And then, just when we were set to tip-toe quietly into settled life, I got a phone call at work one day and we were forced to think again.

DAY 5

FRIDAY JUNE 10:

PASS THE SUN-BLOCK

This morning, the small gap in the curtain said 'blue skies' and for the first time since we arrived, we really suffered in the heat. Head to toe in sun-block, I found the hardest part of the session wasn't so much the running as the recovery, filling your lungs with hot air when they were gasping for a breeze that was cold. Constant thirst was another problem: because of the difficulties we will encounter in taking water on board during the games, Jack doesn't want us gorging ourselves in training. But again, if you want to get the quality into your work, you need to watch your fluid levels. You can't be running around with your tongue hanging out.

A couple of the lads began to get very hot and tired toward the end. Cass twinged his calf, then Stan (Steve Staunton) walked off, complaining about his groin – not that he expected us to believe him. While we all burn, Stan has to take extra special care that the sun doesn't make a mess of him and he obviously felt he had had enough. In a morning of firsts, today was also the first time we learnt about the way we will play. While 4–5–1 has worked well enough for us in the warm-up games, I do wonder a bit if it will prove as effective for us here. Recently, in the games against Holland and Germany, we used Packie to kick a lot of balls high for Tommy and Cass, hoping their defence would head it down to the five-man arc we had formed in midfield. Now while this does work well, it can be very hit and miss and you do run the risk of conceding possession. 'Keep doing it, keep doing it and one will eventually drop for you' is the motto back home, but given the energy you waste in 'doing it' (closing the opposition down) in this heat, is it one we should adopt out here? Because if there was one lesson to emerge from the session today, it is that possession is absolutely everything. So I've been thinking – rather than pump the ball forward against Italy and Mexico, maybe it would be better for Packie to throw a bit more to the full-backs to make them work a bit more. If this hasn't been suggested by the end of next week, I will mention it at one of the sessions.

As my mind began to focus a bit more on the opening game, the other area of wonder concerned who the 1 in the 4–5–1 would be. With Cass joining Aldo (sore knee) and David Kelly (back) and Kev (hamstring) on the injured list today, and eight days to go before the Italy game, Tommy (Coyne) – the least experienced internationally of the three – is the only one of our strikers who is fully fit to play. As to who will fill the other positions against Italy, it's hard to call. While some are already pretty well set out (having played reasonably well in the warm-up games, I'm confident I will keep my place), others have still to be nailed down. But while the debates will continue in the pubs at home as to whether we should play Denis (Irwin) or Gary Kelly, or Jason (McAteer), or Ray (Houghton), or whether the two centre halves should be Phil (Babb) and Alan (Kernaghan) or Paul (McGrath) and Alan, or Paul and Kev, it isn't something we discuss among ourselves. We leave all that to Jack.

Work for the day over, after lunch we drove straight from the training ground to one of Orlando's most popular theme parks, Universal Studios, where we were given the full VIP. On arrival, after posing first for a photograph with Fred, Barney and Wilma – aka the Flintstones – the party split into three and we were brought straight to the top of this massive queue, waiting to experience 'Back to the Future', the most fantastic simulated car ride. While the exclusive treatment was nice, I must say that it was also a bit embarrassing. I mean, having queued there twice while on holiday these last two years, you don't mind stepping back to let disabled people through, but twenty-two fit and healthy track-suited Irishman? No, definitely a bit rich. I know what I would have thought: 'Oi, what's going on here? There's nothing wrong with them.' But anyway, back to the pleasures of the ride – or so to speak. There were eight of us in the DeLorean – Denis, John Sheridan, Cass and Ray in the front and myself, Kev, Aldo and Phil Babb in the back. As the doors close, this garage that was all around you suddenly disappears and before you know it you are flying through space. Now, because I had experienced it twice before and knew exactly what was waiting around each corner, I thought I would be disappointed third time around, but not at all. The thrill, this time, was in the reaction of the others....

Cass: 'Oooh shiiit!'

Aldo: 'Fuuucking 'ell!'

Listening, I was absolutely killing myself.

After 'Jaws' and 'Kongfruntation', which were always going to suffer in comparison, Mick informed us we would be eating at the 'Rock Hard Cafe'. He meant the Hard Rock, of course. Typical Mick!

⚽   ⚽   ⚽

Big Lawrie's leather chair

In January of 1985, five months before Jackie and I were due to marry, Bryan Godfrey, the manager of Weymouth, rang me at work. 'Look,' he said, 'I've just had a phone call from Lawrie McMenemy. Southampton want to buy you.'

'You're joking.' He wasn't. 'Andy, seriously, that is a great club. Believe me, that is a very, very, very good club. You've only got to look at the names in there: Peter Shilton, Mick Mills, Joe Jordan, Mark Wright, Steve Moran, Danny Wallace. They're just oozing international players, quality players. It's a lovely club and I think it would be perfect for you. Why not have a go, son?'

I couldn't quite believe what I was hearing: 'Bryan... I've got to think about this.'

'Well, think about it, but Lawrie wants to talk to you. Can I give him this number?'

'Yeah, okay then.'

The moment I put down the phone, it immediately dawned on me what this was about. It was a wind-up. The lads in the office who knew I played football were winding me up. And I was swallowing it, going for it good and proper. I was still paralysed in my chair ten minutes later, when the phone sounded again and there was this broad Geordie accent down the line.

'I'd like you to come down and meet me,' he said. 'Come down to Southampton. I'd like to talk to you. How do you feel about joining us? Think you could do it?' I was thinking: 'Hell it's him. Or is it? What should I call him? Lawrie? Too informal. Mr McMenemy? Hell, too much of a mouthful. Don't call him anything, don't commit yourself. It's not him at all. But what if it is?'

'Er, yeah, I do think I could do it. Yeah.'

'Would you be willing to move down and give it a go?'

('The Hit. It's coming. I know it's coming. As soon as I agree to go down, the office is going to explode – but the voice, the accent, so authentic. What if it's him?')

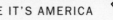

'Yeah. Yeah I would.'

'Okay, well come to the ground tomorrow afternoon and we'll talk about it.'

'Okay. See you then. Cheers.'

Carefully replacing the receiver, I looked around... nothing.

Jackie was my first call, thirty seconds later. Buzzing with enthusiasm I said: 'Jack, think about it. This isn't Bournemouth, this isn't the Third Division we are talking about here. It's Southampton, the team lying sixth in the first. And they want me down there, not on a schoolboy's promise or as an apprentice, but as a professional. I've spoken to Lawrie McMenemy, not some youth-team manager or his secretary but Lawrie bloody McMenemy.'

She was stunned, reserved. I didn't want her to be stunned. I wanted encouragement, direction. I wanted her to say, 'Andy this is a great chance, you *have* to take it.' What I didn't want was what I was read-ing in her silence – the echo of my own thoughts: 'Andy we've just bought a house... are decorating at the moment. We're getting married in five months' time. I've got my friends, my job. So have you. Things just couldn't be better for either of us now. Why take a chance? Why spoil it?' We agreed to talk about it later. I booked a day's leave and arranged to meet Bryan Godfrey at noon the following day. Work over, Mum and Dad were next on my list. Dad was... well, Dad: 'Well, it's up to you son, you know.' Mum, on the other hand, was Jackie: 'I'm not going to tell you not to do it, but think hard about it, Andy. Every-thing you've got around you at the moment is lovely for you, rosy.'

'Think hard about it.' I did that all right. Lying in bed, staring at the ceiling, I thought of nothing else. Jackie, our house, my job, I had been in it five years now, had gone up the ranks, was earning good money, was actually enjoying the work. Throw in my football – part time – and the odd game of snooker, and it's true – life wasn't just rosy, it couldn't be better. And yet, I wanted to do it. I wanted to hear: 'Yeah, go on, do it. Go down there and give it a try'

Bryan was waiting when I stepped off the train. We crossed the road to a cafe and sat down for a chat over a cup of tea. I desperately needed my cards marked before heading to the ground. What sort of man was Lawrie McMenemy? What was he likely to say? Bryan, a former captain of Aston Villa, was well qualified to offer an opinion. 'Lawrie is a straight fellow. He's respected and a nice man as well. He's had some good reports on you and seems satisfied with what he's seen. He'll probably offer you a three-year deal.'

'Yeah Bryan, but what will I ask for? I mean, the money I'm getting from Weymouth and my job…. I'm doing quite well, and if I have to come down here and start from scratch?'

'Well,' he said, 'I'd only be lying to you if I started mentioning numbers. Go and see him, but don't sign anything until you've come back to me.'

I got off to a bad start as soon as I arrived at The Dell. Slipping in through the wrong entrance, I bumped into one of the players, Mark Wright (one of my closest friends today), whose look said, 'Who the hell are you?' Directed to reception, I was led straight to the manager's office. The first thing that struck me about Lawrie McMenemy was his size. A big, imposing fellow, he stood up from his leather chair and offered a hand. 'How are you son, alright?' he asked, looking me up and down.

'Fine thanks,' I meekly replied.

'Good. Well, you can take that out for a start.'

Cripes, my ear-ring! I completely forgot.

'Right,' he continued, 'we've had a few reports on you, and I've taken a look myself but didn't think you played that well.' (Oh cheers. I'm sitting opposite, twiddling my thumbs, nodding my head.) 'But we need some young players and we'd like you to sign. We'll give you a three-year contract so you have plenty of time to settle down, and I won't ask anything of you between now [January] and the end of the season. We've got some big players down here, some of the best players in the country in our dressing-room and although you're coming to us late and have missed out on some of your early years, I'd like to think that once you've settled in you'll be able to show us what you can do.'

I nodded furiously 'Yeah, great, fine,' agreed with every word. Then we came to the crunch. Passing a piece of paper across the desk he said: 'We'll pay you that, for three years.' I picked up the sheet, knew exactly what I wanted it to say – '£400 a week', and I'd have signed there and then. Predictably, however, the figure preceding the noughts was two. Having registered my disappointment as I gazed at the sheet, he continued: 'Now, where are you living at the moment, son?'

'I live in a place called Bexleyheath. We've just actually bought our first house.'

'Yeah? And how much did you pay for that?'

'It cost us £35,000.'

'Thirty five? You'll get a very nice house down here for that. Very nice.'

My spirits down in my toes, I felt like saying, 'Yeah, but my fiancée's working; she ain't going to get a job down here,' but I didn't have the bottle. I felt like saying '£200 pounds a week is not enough. I'm earning more than that now, not to mention the £400 quid a month my girlfriend is bringing in.' But again, I didn't have the nerve.

'Can I have the night to think about it?' I asked.

'Sure,' he replied. 'You go home and speak it over with your girl-friend, but call me by eleven o'clock tomorrow to let me know one way or the other.'

With that, we shook hands again and I left. Bryan was waiting for me out in the car park. 'Look Bryan,' I said, handing him the paper. 'They've offered me that.'

'Well, I know what their attitude is. They're not going to throw everything at you from the start. You're going to have to earn it. And you can, I think you can.'

So I said: 'Well look, mate, I've got to think about this. Drop me back to the station and I'll phone you in the morning.'

'Yeah, have a think about it, okay.'

Back in Bexleyheath, Mum could tell from the hang of my head that it had not gone well. 'Whaaat? You're joking! You're earning more than that now. You've been in that job for five years; what are you toss-ing it away for? And your lifestyle? And the house? And Jackie. You're getting married, she's going to have to come out of her job and go down with you. Andy, think about what you are going to do.'

She was right, of course, but the truth stings. 'Mum,' I snapped, 'I've got ten hours to think about what I am going to do.' Then I left to pick up Jackie and we drove to 'our' new house. The rooms were bare and hollow: we sat on stripped floorboards with our backs to the wall.

Needing to argue my case I started…. 'Jackie, I really want to do this. I really do. I can't help it. If I don't, I know at some stage I'll regret it. I know the money is not much, but that was difficult for me. I wasn't in a position to turn around and say, 'That's not enough, I want more.' I was shocked, I really thought they'd offer more.' But I was wasting my breath, for Jackie had already decided that she wasn't going to stand in my way. Feeling a bit better, we locked up, went home and the night went easier with me.

There was an unexpected bonus when I phoned Southampton next morning. 'What I forgot to tell you yesterday is,' Lawrie McMenemy said, as soon as he picked up the phone, 'we'll give you five thousand quid to sign.'

'Okay, that will be great,' I replied, delighted with the cushion, 'because I've thought about it and I want to do it.'

'Good. Can you get yourself down here for a medical so we can sign the contract?'

'I can, but I don't know what sort of notice I've got to serve in work.' Immediately, he got his secretary to contact my office and the standard month's notice was reduced to two weeks. Two days later, I travelled down for the medical and the signing of the contract. There was just one minor detail to be sorted before signing on the bottom line.

'Look,' I said. 'There's just one small thing. I'm getting married on May the eleventh and the season doesn't end until May. Now, I'm not presuming for one second that I'm going to be involved [in the first team] – in fact, I'm sure I won't be, but I have to make one point clear; there is no way I can go home and tell my girlfriend we have to post-pone it on the chance that I might be. I mean I'm not sure what it's like down here, but it's crazy up in London. We've had to book everything a year in advance.'

'Well, all right,' he replied. 'I don't think it will be a problem. We'll cross that bridge when we come to it.'

Happy, I signed.

 **DAY 6**

SATURDAY JUNE 11:

WHEN THE CAT'S AWAY...

09:00 A quick poll at breakfast, 'Is everybody feeling absolutely knackered this morning or is it just me?' confirms the difficulty I have in walking from my bed to the lift to the breakfast table. Five days of heavy training are beginning to leave a trace.

10:00 With Mexico playing Northern Ireland in a friendly tonight, Jack handed the training duties to his assistant Maurice Setters and took a flight to Miami to watch the game. On another scorching day, the first steps of the session confirm the weariness at breakfast. Ploddy and labouring, we are twenty-two flat batteries in need of charge.

10:30. Warmed up and stretched off, we notice the cracks beginning to appear as soon as we start to sweat. Perhaps the biggest problem of performing in this heat which I did not mention yesterday is its tendency to make you irritable. While there were traces creeping in towards the end of yesterday's session, it seems more pronounced today. Players are snapping at each other.

10:45 Given that we all get on so well together, at first it strikes me as unusual when the abuse begins to hurl around. Because of our involvement at club level, when an international might be squeezed between two weekend games, training is normally light whenever we meet in Dublin. Make a mistake in a five-a-side at home and someone might make a joke, but would very rarely scream. But here, in this hundred-plus heat that parches your throat and threatens to melt down your brain, when to lose it means to chase it, you daren't make a mistake. 'For fuck's sake, can't you keep hold of the damn thing!' because here, the ball is precious.

11:00 Not that the younger lads – the Gary Kellys, the Jasons, the Phil Babbs – would ever dream of 'having a go'. It's not their place yet, is it? You need caps under you belt – to be a Ronnie (Whelan) or a Ray or a Stan – before you earn the right to scream. Give them another year no doubt....

11:45 The session ends – a good morning's work. Although the pot has simmered on occasion, the lid is still in place as we walk from the field. A shower, lunch and the cool, air-conditioned rest rooms of the pavilion restore the natural good humour. Indeed, if we could return immediately to the hotel and snooze for the afternoon, everything would be positively dandy. Alas, our little treat was yesterday (Universal Studios) and Jack has left instructions that we must train twice today. So at 13:45, fed and watered, we lace up again. But there's not much spring in our strides when we step out into the heat.

14:00 This is what ignited the flame: after the customary warm-up and stretch, a nine-a-side is organised using the full length of the pitch. Normally, it must be explained, only the width of the pitch is used, a tighter playing area making for a tighter, sharper game, and though we point this out to Maurice, he's not interested. Now in fairness, maybe he's only carrying out instructions, maybe Jack has told him he wants the soles run off our feet on the bigger field, but given the temperature of the afternoon and the general state of fatigue, it doesn't make sense at all. And we say so. Alas, to no avail.

14:30 Feet burning, lungs heaving, I sprint down the left touch-line with the ball at my feet and, looking up, spot Niall (Quinn) moving with me down the right. Swinging over my cross (not one of my better ones I admit), I watch in despair as he connects but fails to control. 'For fuck's sake Quinny,' I scream, with what feels like a dying breath. But he's not finished yet. Over in the corner he has managed to retrieve the ball. 'Still in,' he roars, turning towards the target. 'Naah, that's gone,' the defenders counter – they would, wouldn't they? The squabbling continues, the game breaks down and we look to Maurice for a decision. 'Goal kick,' he announces, from his position on the halfway line.

'How the fuck can you see from there?' I argue, incensed, the heat starting to get to me.

'Get on with it,' he replies, not interested.

14:35 The game degenerates with every minute that passes. The pitch is too big, players are knackered, walking. Impossible to get near enough to close the opposition down. With enough, clearly enough, I turn to Maurice and suggest he ends the game: 'Look, I don't think any of us are benefiting from this. I know the objective is to try and get everyone fit, but I don't think this is doing anyone any good. Everybody is knackered, Maurice.' But again, he is not interested: 'Just get on with it.' At this stage, I lose control. Say things I later regret. Obscenities are exchanged. Some other players join in. Feeling is still running high when we eventually leave the field.

16:00   I've been thinking about this a lot since I returned to the hotel, and if it had been Jack out there today. Would we have had a go at him the way we had a go at Maurice? I'm not sure. Perhaps not. It's one of the problems all assistants face in being number two. I remember my time at Southampton, the five-a-sides, the way the games seemed faster whenever Lawrie was around. Lawrie McMenemy was a man-manager; liked to talk, listen, always commanded respect. Not that respect has much to do with it. We liked and respected his assistant, Lew Chatterley as well – he was a good fellow and yet, whenever he had control of the team, our attitude completely changed.

'Come on Andy get moving.'

'Naff off Lew, give us a break.' Because although he was technically in charge, it was temporary. Lawrie was the number one, Lawrie was the power. You put a spring in your step when he was around – but not for Lew. And at every other club I've played for, it's been exactly the same.

19:00   Maurice has the hump, wasn't talking over dinner, and though I feel I should apologise, there was wrong on both sides. Jack wouldn't have let things run in the way that Maurice did today, but I suppose what I said was a bit out of order. I'll have a quiet word with him... later.

22:00   Have hit the bed early tonight, just popped a 'sleeper'. If Jackie could see me now.... Saturday nights in Bexleyheath were never anything like this.

Tea and tears at Waterloo

Driving to the ground to begin my first day at work, I can't say I was actually smitten by a spirit of adventure. There was no fairytale crap in my head: 'This is the chance I've always been waiting for, now I'm going to show the world.' No I was anxious, scared, still wondering if I was doing the right thing. I mean, if, a year or two down the road, Lawrie McMenemy had turned around and said: 'Ahh, well, at least you've had a go, hard luck son,' then it would have been hard luck because jobs were getting hard to come by and I'd have tossed away five years of a profession. And yet in other ways I was looking forward to it. Andy Townsend, professional footballer, did have a certain ring to it, and I was curious to find out what the game at the very top was all about.

The Dell was pretty deserted. Most of the pros report directly to the training ground, and after being introduced to Lew Chatterley, Dave Merrington the youth-team manager and Don Taylor the physio, I watched a few of the apprentices (Alan Shearer and Matt Le Tissier would have been among them) playing snooker, until it was time to get on the bus.

'Are you the new signing?' one of the apprentices asked.

'Yeah.'

'And where have you come [signed] from?'

'Weymouth.'

'Oh.'

It clearly went down a bomb.

Out at the training ground, an apprentice – 'my' apprentice (that was a pleasant surprise) – handed me a kit with the number 35, then took away my boots to label them correspondingly so he would know them for cleaning and polishing. Taking the kit, I was pointed in the direction of the reserve-team dressing-room. Being introduced to faces that meant very little to me, I sat down and was subjected to the usual mickey-taking. 'No, you can't sit there that's so-and-so's peg.' Stripped and ready, I sat touching my toes, nervous and tense, building myself up as if I was about to play a major game. In a way, I was. First impressions are important. The last thing you want is to have a nightmare on your first day.

Training began with a communal jog. The big boys – the Mills, the Shiltons – were here now and had wished me luck walking out on the field. The warm-up over, Lew Chatterley took the first-team boys off to another part of the ground and I was left with Dennis Rofe, who managed the reserves. Not to have been thrown in at the deep end was a huge relief. Although the session was light and didn't cause me too many problems, that night when I returned to my digs I was mentally drained.

Three weeks later I was on a train bound for London. After a relatively calm opening day, my fortunes with the reserves had taken a turn. Jackie was coming straight from work and we were going to talk about it at the station. Waterloo – how appropriate. I needed to talk, needed to thrash it out. Then I could make up my mind if I wanted to return.

As a rule, I've always tried to be honest with myself. From my earliest days, I've never had to be told when I've played badly and when I've played well. As I sat, reflecting, on the train to London, I was in no doubt at all how the first three games of my professional career had gone. Badly. Very badly. So badly that I couldn't understand what was wrong. At Weymouth, a month earlier, I'd been 'the man', the top dog. At Weymouth the cry was: 'Give the ball to Andy, *he'll* score us a goal.' But here at Southampton, among the sixteen and seventeen-year-olds who thought they were better than me, who were playing better than me, it must have been: 'Look at him, he's got no chance, no chance.'

Problem is, after a while you begin to think it yourself. Three bad games and you're walking off thinking: 'I'm a million miles from playing for Southampton, I've got no chance.' And once you begin creeping into your shell, the second-thought syndrome sets in: 'I shouldn't have bothered. Why did I do it?' until before you know it, you're not only thinking it but believing it. And believing it is dangerous. Once that starts, you're gone. I was pretty close to gone on the day I phoned Jackie. It was crisis time; the first I had had in my life.

My opening game hadn't been great. It wasn't a catastrophe, I didn't embarrass myself or anything, but I didn't shine. At first I thought the extra running I'd been putting in at training was the cause, so I eased off, hoping the spark would return. But my performance in the second game was no better than the first, and in the third no better than the second. By the time of the fourth game, I was having serious doubts. Not that Dennis Rofe or anyone at the club had said anything; I hadn't had any bollockings. No 'This is the real world, Townsend, now get your finger out!' I don't know, it was just a rut that seemed to get deeper the harder I tried to climb out.

Being in digs didn't help. The family I was staying with couldn't have been nicer, and my room was well furnished and comfortable. But it wasn't *my* room. They weren't *my* family. I needed a hug, a shoulder, reassurance; things I couldn't talk about on the phone in their front room. So I'd go outside, spend a fortune in the call box, first telling my parents that I was loving it and getting on fine and then telling Jackie the complete opposite. It dragged on for a week... three weeks, until finally, one Wednesday, I cracked before a game. Struggling with a bruised calf, I had assured Dennis Rofe at training the day before that I'd be fit enough to play. And I probably would have been, if I hadn't bumped into Lew Chatterley a couple of hours before the game.

I was about to walk to the gym for a last-minute fitness test, when he asked: 'Is your leg all right? I want to have a look at you tonight.'

Stunned, I replied: 'You want to have a look at *me*?'

'Yeah, you're playing tonight aren't you? I want to watch you in some detail.'

'Well, I'm not sure Lew. This calf is bloody sore. I'm not sure I'll make it.'

'Oh. Okay, if you're not fit, don't play.'

And I didn't. Later that evening, as I sat and watched the game, I might easily have been back in my mother's front room in Bexleyheath, a nine-year-old boy struggling to come to terms with his weakness. Then it had been a penalty kick, this time, a game – but the guilt and self-disgust felt exactly the same. I thought: 'I cannot believe you did that. I cannot believe you bottled out of playing in this game! What on earth were you thinking of? You've come here to play football, to try and make it as a professional... and here you are, ducking out of playing for the reserves.' The following day I phoned Jackie and asked her to meet me off the train.

In hindsight, perhaps being pitched straight into the reserves wasn't the healthiest thing that could have happened to me. It's not that the reserve team was a breeding ground for depression or anything: reserve-team players like their joke and their laugh the same as first-team players. Indeed, reserve-team dressing-rooms are almost as lively and bubbly as first-team dressing-rooms. Almost. The difference is subtle but important. Simmering beneath the apparent good humour is an attitude problem: none of them play in the first team, all believe they should.

Playing with the reserves isn't easy: encouraged to believe you're (an important) part of the family, you've been shunned by a father who clearly prefers your brother, who doesn't think you're good enough, who won't give you a game. As a result, bad attitudes reign: 'Bloody place... this is a shit-hole... don't know why I've come here. And it's understandable: no one should be content with being part of the furniture. Football is nothing unless you're playing in the first team. But again, this is hindsight: what is clear and simple to me now was so confusing and frustrating back then.

Jackie was waiting as I stepped on to the platform. As soon as I saw her, I thought I was going to cry. We took refuge at a nearby cafe, ordered some tea and for the next two hours the floodgates opened as three weeks of tension and frustration poured out. Jackie was shocked. In the six or seven years we had known each other, I had always been the 'rock', the wise-cracking, confident guy. She had never seen me in such a fragile, tearful state.

'Don't worry about it,' she said, 'you're not the first player this has ever happened to and you're certainly not going to be the last. I know you're feeling low at the moment, but I'll be down there with you soon. Calm down, everything will be okay.'

'No Jack,' I blurted, 'you don't understand. I want to do well... and I've done nothing. I haven't done anything really at the moment. I'm not playing half as well as I was when I was playing part-time football and here I am, supposed to be a professional.'

'Yes but it doesn't have to happen overnight – you've signed for three years for goodness sake. Take it easy, give yourself time.'

It was all I needed to hear. Not that I was exactly light of step when it came to leaving her and getting back on the train. Feeling like a soldier heading off to war, I would have loved to have turned my back on it there and then. But quitting wasn't an option. I trained as normal the next day. A letter from Jackie arrived a day later. In the week that followed, I rediscovered my perspective and the 'mountain' was once again a 'molehill'.

The breakthrough was a reserve-team game against Luton. On a Saturday at The Dell, I had a right ding-dong battle with Gary Parker (today a team-mate at Villa) and scored the second goal – a cracking drive from 30 yards – in a 2–1 win. Walking off the pitch, I knew I had done well and at last felt I was delivering on my talent. Encouraged on the training ground by the prompting of Mark Wright and Mark Dennis, it wasn't long before I began hoping to join them in the first team. Two not inconsiderable obstacles stood in my way. The first was Southampton's position in the League: fluctuating between fifth and sixth in the table, the team were driving, rather than coasting to the end of the season and, with a place in Europe the carrot, this wasn't a time for introducing new blood. The second was the man holding down my position. Though beginning to wind down his career, England international David Armstrong was far from over the hill and still a bloody good player. Having forked out six hundred and fifty grand (a lot of money ten years ago) for his services, there was no way Lawrie McMenemy was going to replace him with an inexperienced left-footer he'd found in the bargain basement at Weymouth. And yet, despite the odds, I didn't give up hope. Confidence totally restored, I could do it. I knew I could do it. Wanted to do it so bad that on Saturdays, when the reserves weren't playing, I'd trip along to The Dell and follow Dave's every stride like a hawk for the afternoon – 'Oops, that wasn't so clever' – convincing myself each time that I'd have done better. What I didn't envisage, of course, was the possibility we might play together.

The first inkling I had that my status was about to change was a few weeks later at training, when Lawrie not only attended the session but arrived with his track suit on. While he's an excellent man-manager, if there is one thing Lawrie McMenemy has never been it's a track-suit manager, so for him to turn up in football boots was unusual to say the least. Enjoying the smirks and giggles (he was really quite a sight), I thought no more of it and was told to fall in with the big boys. Again, there was nothing unusual in this as I had trained with them a number of times before on Thursdays. It was after the warm-up when the game of shadow play – knocking the ball around in position with no opposition or physical contact – was organised that I began to suspect. It was primarily an exercise in familiarisation, and as I stood, surrounded by the Peter Shiltons and Joe Jordans, I didn't need to be Einstein to work out that the only one in need of it was me. The penny dropped. Mark Dennis had been suspended after a booking the Saturday before. I was the only other natural left-footer in the squad. *He was going to play me in Mark's position. He was going to play me at left back!* Delighted, I was also suddenly afraid. I'd never played at left back in my life.

The (shadow) game began. As I was peeling off to the touchline, 'pretending' to make myself available, 'Shilts' threw me the ball. Taking it, I looked up and knocked it down the line to Joe Jordan then ran forward to support as it came back to midfield. Sprinting now... left...

right... all over the place, I was buzzing with enthusiasm, mad keen to impress – until Lawrie called me over and stopped the game. 'Calm down son,' he said. 'You haven't got to go mad playing this position. Take it easy, you're all right. I'm not asking you to be a left back. Get as tight as you like to the man in front of you – if anything goes over your head, the centre half [we played with three] nearest you will take care of it. So just slow down, relax.'

Relax? He must have been joking. Racing out of the ground as soon as training finished, I had some calls to make, people to tell.

'Dad? Mark Dennis is suspended and I've been training with the first team today. I think they're looking to play me on Saturday against Villa.'

'Oh really?'

'Yeah, so get ready, get everyone on standby to come down to the game.'

Saturday April 20: I remember my debut game – all footballers do. It becomes a blur after that; seasons come and go, the sponsors on your shirt change, but the day-to-day routine of the job on matchdays is always the same. It wasn't a job back then – not on my debut game. It was fast, exciting, a day of so many firsts.

'What would you like to eat, sir?' the waiter at the Polygon enquired. I felt almost embarrassed ordering eggs and beans. Pre-match meals were a first. With the reserves, the attitude was 'eat what you want whenever you want, just make sure you're at the ground an hour before the game'. But this was class. Serious. A completely different world. Pasta? Potatoes? Steak? Rice pudding? Your every whim was catered for. Out at The Dell, the star treatment continued. We were mobbed as we stepped off the coach, and it was almost a thrill to sign autographs. In my four months at the club, my contract had been the only time I'd been asked to sign my name. Inside, my boots – polished and shining – had been placed neatly under the peg holding a crisp new number three shirt. 'Would you like a rub on your legs?' the physio asked. Hmm, that made me laugh. If I'd asked him two weeks earlier, he'd have said, 'Bollocks, rub them yourself.' So many firsts, so many firsts....

Ten minutes before kick-off, the manager came over for a quick word: 'Okay son? Feel up to it?'

'Yeah I do.' I replied.

'Right then, good luck. Now you're not a left back, you're not a defender but just join in whenever you can. Don't worry about anything behind you. If you see a danger, let it be in front of you and go and confront it there.'

The buzzer sounded; my team-mates wished me luck and we left the dressing-room. Tripping down the little flight of stairs, we ran out in the corner on to the pitch. First impressions were of this sea of heads – The Dell had always been empty when I'd played with the reserves and I couldn't get over the size of the crowd, fifteen, sixteen thousand heads all looking in. The view looked so different when you were one of eleven looking out. Straight away, I scanned the area where the players' wives normally sat to try and pick out Jackie, but I couldn't see her. I tried to find my dad and brothers but couldn't see them either: their car had broken down on the way from London and they would miss the opening half hour.

From the moment we kicked off, I felt comfortable and relaxed. Tony Daley, who was also making his debut, was running at me for the afternoon but I managed to keep him quiet (I must have been fast in those days). I couldn't have picked a better day to pull off my best performance since arriving at the club. Ninety minutes later, the relief I felt at having not let anyone down meant more to me than the 2–0 win. I'll never forget the crowd as we walked off the pitch, the lads in the dressing-room slapping me on the back, Lawrie coming in and saying, 'Well played kid, very well done.' It was a brilliant, brilliant day.

I showered and changed into my shirt and tie, joined Jackie, my dad and Mike and Ken in the players' lounge for a drink, then rushed out to read the report in the Saturday sports edition of the local paper or the 'Pink 'un' as it was called. 'As good a Southampton debut as I can remember', it said. Bet he's written that a couple of times since. Later, when I took Jackie out for a meal, she couldn't resist a couple of 'I-told-you-sos.' We laughed. My train ride to London seemed a million miles away.

On Monday, it was back to earth with a bump. Subjected to some over-the-top bollockings from Lew at the training ground, I forgave him when he informed me I would be travelling with the team next day to Manchester and then on to Newcastle for a game on Saturday. When we arrived at the team hotel, on the afternoon of the United game, I wasn't that surprised when Lawrie came over and told me he was putting Mark Dennis back in the team. I didn't even expect I'd make the substitutes' bench – and I didn't. 'But,' he reminded me, 'you played well the other day, didn't do yourself any harm at all. You've set the standard down, now you've got to keep it.'

Old Trafford was impressive – three times the size of The Dell. Taking my place in the dug-out beside Lew Chatterley, who was the sponge man as well as Lawrie's assistant, I watched as United kicked off and Bryan Robson lobbed this ball forward for Mark Hughes to run on to in our box. Our Mark (Dennis), got there first but was felled in the clash with Hughes, whose knee crashed into Dennis' thigh. Now, in order to make clear what happened next, at this stage I must explain that Mark Dennis, as well as being a top-class defender, was also one of the real characters of the team and forever taking the mickey out of Lew. All season they had this running joke between them where, every time he went down injured, Mark would wait until Lew – sprinting off the bench like a lunatic – was within ten feet before jumping up and telling him he needn't have bothered.

So anyway, twenty seconds into the game, Mark went down after the clash with Hughes and Lew, who hadn't seen the clash, thought he was faking: 'I'm not going out. He's taking the piss. As soon as I run out, he'll jump up and make me look a right prat.' So we sat and watched for a minute. Mark, raising his arm, was gesturing wildly by now: 'Oi, get on. I'm fuckin' hurt.' So Lew ran out and gave him some treatment and Mark managed to play out the 0–0 draw – never a bad result at Old Trafford. Back at the hotel after the game, spirits were high and after a quick bite of food, we congregated in the bar for a couple of beers. Now by this stage, Mark Dennis' thigh was beginning to swell seriously and Lew, concerned about Saturday's game, was rabbiting on at him to go back to his room and put some ice on it. But the fun was only just starting and Mark wasn't interested: 'Leave off Lew, I've got through the game. I'm not sitting in the room on my own; I just want to have a couple of drinks with the lads.'

'All right, suit yourself,' Lew sighed, and walked off to bed.

I followed myself shortly after, nodded off to sleep, then was woken in the middle of the night by a commotion in the corridor. The following morning, the breakfast table was buzzing with news of Mark and what had disturbed me. Anaesthetised by the alcohol as he trotted off to bed, what he didn't realise was that the swelling around his thigh was a haematoma. At four o'clock in the morning – climbing up the walls now that the painkilling beer had worn off – he decided to phone for help. 'I was prepared to help you four hours ago but now you can go and bollocks,' Lew told him, suspecting another prank. So Mark called an ambulance himself and was immediately rushed to hospital, where the throbbing mass was slit open as soon as he arrived, leaving him with a scar the length of his knee – and out for the rest of the season. In the most bizarre circumstances possible, I was suddenly back in the team!

Although we lost the Newcastle game 2–1, the run-in to the end of the season went well for both me and the team and we needed three points from our last two fixtures – home to Coventry and Liverpool – to secure our place in Europe. While I was delighted to be finishing the season as a first-team regular, a prior engagement on the day of the Coventry game left me with an unbelievable dilemma....

The negotiation started on Monday.

'Boss, you do remember back in January when I signed the contract I spoke to you about my wedding?'

'Riiight.' Sounding very unsure.

'Well, it's next Saturday. I'm getting married next Saturday and I know this is a bad time and I know what you are going to say to me, but I've got 150 people turning up and the hotel has been booked for over a year and if I don't turn up at that church at three o'clock, I'm basically going to have my throat cut.'

'Well, I appreciate your difficulties, but I've got a UEFA Cup spot to go for, son, and you've been playing and your priorities are here.' And he looked at me. At that moment I can remember almost trembling with panic: 'Oh please God, help me convince this man that this has cost my mother-in-law and father-in-law an arm and a leg and that I can't just turn around and ask Jackie if we can postpone it for a couple of weeks.'

Desperate now, I said: 'I'm sorry, I can't, I've got to go. Look, I know it's letting you down, but I did say when I joined that I needed that Saturday, and that Saturday is next Saturday and I need it. I can't back out of it. I can't do it.'

'All right,' he said, changing his tone to one of compromise. 'I'll speak to you again about it later in the week.' So I left the office no wiser than when I had walked in.

Later that evening Jackie, in the great tradition of brides in their wedding week, was more than a little crisp when I informed her of the state of play. 'What do you mean you *think* it will be all right? You do realise that people will be sitting down, that there's 150 meals being dished up next Saturday at five o'clock.' Tuesday and Wednesday passed without a word, and when an effort to enlist Lew Chatterley as a

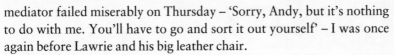

mediator failed miserably on Thursday – 'Sorry, Andy, but it's nothing to do with me. You'll have to go and sort it out yourself' – I was once again before Lawrie and his big leather chair.

'Boss? About Saturday... are you going to let me go?'

He smiled: 'Yeah okay.'

'Oh great, thanks very much.'

'But I want you back first thing on Sunday morning, because we've got Liverpool on Tuesday and that's a very important game for us.'

'Okay, of course. First thing Sunday morning.' I could have kissed the great man's feet.

The wedding went well; Jackie's uncles and aunts kept me informed about the latest score from The Dell and a 2–1 win for Southampton meant I could relax and enjoy the evening. Next morning, a little the worse for wear, we were up at seven for the drive to Southampton and I reported back for duty at nine. Lawrie put me back in the side for the game against Liverpool but, pitted against players of the calibre of Dalglish and Rush and still slightly weary from carrying my new wife across the threshold, I did not play one of my better games. 'I think you learned a little bit about what it's *really* all about tonight, didn't you, son?' Lawrie suggested when it was over. Not that I was too disappointed; the point secured against Liverpool (1–1) meant we had qualified for Europe and celebration was the order of the night. Not that we would ever get to play there. The horrific evening waiting just around the corner would see to that: Liverpool, Juventus, Heysel.

The summer of '85 was one of the best I had known. The end-of-season tour to Trinidad and Tobago was followed by a late honeymoon to Cyprus, and seven months after abandoning my job at Greenwich Council, I was enjoying a very different style of life. I still, however, had reservations about my take-home pay. Jackie's new job eased the burden of our mortgage repayments, but without it we would have struggled, and I resolved to see Lawrie about a revision as soon as pre-season resumed. If I had known then what I know now, I wouldn't have left it so late. Lawrie, tempted by an offer to return to his native land, moved his big leather chair up north to the ailing Sunderland and took Lew, his faithful assistant, along for the ride. Chris Nicholl, the former Southampton player and Northern Ireland international, was appointed his successor. He was as much a stranger to me as I was to him, and from the first day we sat down, I wasn't sure we would get along.

DAY 7

SUNDAY JUNE 12:

HIDDEN BUNKERS, TOOTHY HAZARDS

Because of the game's late kick-off (Mexico 3 – Northern Ireland 0), we didn't see Jack until breakfast this morning. Maurice was also present. He seemed quiet, and as I sat down to tackle my cereal, I wondered whether Jack would have a word: 'Andy, what on earth is going on? I leave Maurice in charge and you lot start.... ' He didn't. Maurice had obviously not said a word, or he had and Jack had discarded it. The first contact I had with him was when I asked for his impressions of the night before. Although one or two of the Mexican players had impressed, overall he didn't feel Northern Ireland had made it that hard for them. 'They didn't really get about them much, didn't get after them. They've got one or two that are half-decent but they can be got at.'

Rollins College were warmed up and waiting when we went out. Eleven youngsters from the local soccer school – or academy as they say here – had been drafted in to add a touch of spice to our daily routine. As we set off on our warm-up jog, the jokes started flying as we watched them preparing on the other side of the park. One of their players, a coloured lad, looked particularly athletic. I said to Stan: 'Bet he's on your wing, Stan,' but Stan wasn't impressed. 'Oh fuck, a "flyer", that's all I need this morning.' The fact that we were suddenly, unwittingly, focusing on them brought to mind one of the peculiarities of the game that I've noticed over the years. It doesn't matter who the . opposition are – whether it's Germany away in Hanover or Grimsby at home in the FA Cup – you can never resist 'a look' before running out. Germany, when we played them in Hanover recently, were a particularly intimidating lot: chests out, shoulders back, all six feet three. 'These are a big mob,' I thought in the tunnel before the game. But ninety minutes later we had beaten them.

Now Rollins College, while no Germany, were still a good deal better than a team of waiters you might play in Marbella and, as a result, warranted respect. 'Don't go mad,' Jack instructed us on naming his team. 'Just keep it moving, keep it free and get your arses shifting a bit.' The game started. We scored early and they replied, but soon the difference in class told and we ran out comfortable winners. Perhaps the most surprising thing about them was their accents: while we expected to hear total Florida drawl, there was one cockney, another Mancunian, and there may even have been a Scot. One of their players, Gordon Hill, was a familiar blast from the past and, as we walked back to the changing rooms, he told me of his new life. Having failed to find a suitable post in England when he retired from the game, he emigrated to Tampa, Florida, and today his coaching school (academy) caters for 500 kids. 'You should consider it yourself,' he said as we split. I agreed that I would.

Showered, changed, and let off the leash for the remainder of the afternoon (and evening), we quickly returned to the hotel and set about arranging some golf. Now, Jack doesn't want us playing. Has stated all week 'No golf,' so it was very much a case of slipping out the side door once we had ordered two cars. Perhaps we should have asked, but given that we were going to be using buggies and all had hats and blocker to protect us from the sun, rather than make a song and dance about it we decided it would be better just to go.

After eight days of training and routine, it felt great to pull a wood from the bag. The opening hole went well for me: good drive, nice iron, then up and down for a par. But then, as we moved on to the second and I stepped from buggy to tee, I was suddenly thrown off my game. It was the ripples in the lake to the right of the fairway, the two huge eyes floating just above the surface at alarming speed. 'Blimey, an alligator.' Now, ever since I had that chat with Tony – one of the staff at the training ground – alligators have been occupying quite a lot of my vacant thoughts. 'Did you know [not his exact words] they've nabbed little kids playing innocently in their gardens? Did you know they are absolutely wild – that five minutes from here the swamps are crawling with them?'

'No,' I gasped, 'I didn't.'

So anyway, as I stood on the second tee and looked down the fairway (no fence!), these children that have been gobbled in gardens began to affect how I saw the shot. And as I swung and prepared to connect, I was mindful of the toothy hazard to the right and the need to place it left... whaaaaccck... but not that far left. Never mind. Ronnie was next up. Striking powerfully, he sent it off the fairway to the right. 'You can kiss my arse if you think I'm looking for that,' I told him as we set off down the fairway. 'He's behind you,' I screamed as he lined up his second shot. As for me, well, concentration disturbed, I dropped a shot, saved a leg, but was off form for the rest of the round.

We come to bury Sacchi

ITALY
(JUNE 13 TO JUNE 18)

DAY 8

MONDAY JUNE 13:

COUNTDOWN: THE PRESSURE COOKING STARTS HERE

Looking back to the World Cup 1990, it's the traffic as much as the tension that stands out most. We couldn't believe it at first. I mean, you expect traffic in Rome – it's almost as essential a part of the city as the Vatican or the Colosseum – but this was Nemi, not St Peter's Square. A small, unremarkable town some thirty miles outside. Where were all these cars going, blowing their horns and squealing their tyres? Well, nowhere as it turned out. They were just doing their bit for their country, just reminding us why we were here and who we would be playing. *Grazie,* lads, but we hadn't forgotten.

Sleep might have come easier in a classier hotel. We wouldn't have needed the breeze off the street then – could have closed the windows, turned on the AC, and ignored the final laps of the Italian Grand Prix outside. However, this was no Hilton; small rooms, flat food, no satellite or MTV, and an air conditioning system that hadn't been replaced since the fall of Nero. Surely we deserved better? Surely we deserved more on the night before the biggest game in our lives?

Of the game itself, I remember the tension beforehand, the length of the walk to the pitch. In all my time in football, I have never walked so far and, still underground after what seemed half a mile, we began looking around in the hope of flagging a cab. In the dressing-room beforehand, Jack stressed the need for discipline and calm. 'Remember,' he said, 'you are playing this lot in their own back yard and will have everything going against you. The ref is not going to give you an ounce, so don't stand there moaning if decisions don't go your way. They'll be falling over and rolling around and calling and flapping their arms and all that shit, but don't be distracted by it.' Sound advice in the relative cool of the dressing-room, but difficult to implement in the cauldron outside.

I remember, in particular, the theatricals of De Napoli after my (mildly) robust challenge had sent him tumbling to the ground.

Halfway around his fourth or fifth roll, three of his team-mates surrounded the ref and gave exquisite Marcel Marceau performances of how a ref produces his card. So I ran over, and having told them exactly what I thought of their efforts to have me booked, I turned to De Napoli, who by this stage must have been dizzy on the ground. Although I'd barely touched him, his face was wrinkled in agony as if I'd just broken his leg. 'Get up, get up,' I shouted at him – and then he did the most amazing thing. After a quick check that the referee's back was turned, his mask of misery suddenly became one of mirth and, stroking his thumb against his index and middle fingers, he smiled: 'Money, money, money.' Was he alluding to their bonus? Their reward for moving on to the semi-final? To this day, the gesture still puzzles me. I don't know.

When it was over and we had lost, I exchanged shirts with Donadoni – a memento of the quarter-final that I would treasure, along with the Ronald Koeman (Holland) and Mark Wright (England) shirts I had collected in earlier games. Mick McCarthy was outstanding in this department of the game – scooped Baresi's (Italy), Gullit's (Holland), Hagi's (Rumania), all the big names. Cass exchanged his with Vialli; indeed, they seemed to hit it off quite well, later exchanging their track suits as well as we walked towards our respective team buses. Now, if the sight of this very Italian Italian in the green and white (extra extra large) of Ireland looked odd, then Cass really looked the part in Diadora silky blue. 'Perhaps I should go and sit with them on the other coach,' he laughed. 'I've got some shades here in my bag. Do you think I should put them on?'

⚽　　⚽　　⚽

Four years on, Vialli hasn't made it this time, but Baresi and Donadoni have. And Baggio, of course. Today, after seven days of sweating and running and practice, where the enemy has been heat, and the goal how to survive, we at last began to talk about Italy and the opening game of the tournament. The goalkeeper Pagliuca's weaknesses, Signori's free kicks, Baresi's addiction to the off-side trap, Baggio's ability to create... for the next six days these will dominate our lives. Today, the count-down began.

It started with Jack in a foul mood. The *Sun* have interpreted some comment he made about treating us like adults and not monks as a licence to run a story with the headline 'BOOZE ON LADS'. Walking through the foyer on the way to the team bus, I could tell he was not pleased from his tone to John Givens (the press officer): 'They take everything you bloody say and....'

Out at the training ground, on what was undoubtedly the hottest day so far, the opening session went well, with Italy and Roberto Baggio the focus from kick-off. 'They like to play it to him, get it back and let people run in from there,' Jack told us and, to fix this in our minds, he organised a simulation of some of their moves. This is how it worked: Packie, Terry Phelan, Phil Babb, Paul McGrath and Denis Irwin were selected (a sign?) in their normal roles as the Irish back five. Attacking them, myself, John Sheridan and Alan McLaughlin played as if we were Albertini, Dino Baggio and Donadoni and using Jason McAteer, who was clearly delighting in the role of Roberto Baggio. The objective was to try and unhinge – and thus familiarise – our defence with the Italian way. Apart from Jack's impression of Arrigo Sacchi ('What the **** are you doing? Not like that....'), it seemed to work quite well.

After the impersonations of *la squadra*, there was a brief discussion on the off-side trap, where it was agreed for our defenders (who are not short of pace) to stick with their runners, rather than try to box too clever and play for off-side. 'Why take a chance on the fellow sticking his flag up?' Jack asked. 'Why trust a linesman with your bloody life?' Point taken, free-kick practice (starring Denis Irwin as one of the best dead-ball kickers in the world) ended the morning session, and after a shower and a quick bite of lunch, it was back out for round two in the afternoon.

A game was organised on the full length of the pitch. Jack wanted us to be free and easy with the ball and to focus on the means we could employ to survive the impossible heat. Running forward with the ball, we practised stopping, turning and knocking it back to Packie, so that he could put his foot on it, tee it up and earn us all a breather. The art of darting on and off to the sideline for a drink was also rehearsed, Jack observing and probing...

'Do you feel better for the odd drink?'

'Would it be better if we wrapped some ice in towels and threw them on?'

...trying to hone and define the perfect strategy for Saturday's game.

This is a facet of his management that is not generally appreciated – how much of himself he puts into each of these games. Because he always appears so nonchalant, because he is forever joking about fishing and sometimes forgets his squad members' names, people sometimes form the impression that he doesn't really care. He cares all right – cares so much that for the next five days he'll be like a pressure cooker on the boil, rumbling and rattling and hissing until the final whistle on Saturday, when he will light up a cigar and release all the steam. Which is why the 'Booze on' story, and its implication that we are only here for a good time, would have hurt him so much. He wants the team to play well here, better than it has played before. As he says himself, so many people have patted him on the back before coming out, so many people have made presentations and heaped praise, it wouldn't be right to travel out here and be content with what has been achieved before. So he had a go at them – the press – at lunchtime, then warned us all not even to breathe when they were around: 'They chop and change everything.'

This evening, just after dinner, I phoned Jackie at home; tonight, sitting watching the telly, she was feeling a bit fed up. This is a difficult time for the wives. The days, she explains, pass quickly when swimming, doing whatever the kids want to do, but at night, when the kids are in bed, it's not much fun sitting at home alone. As players, we've a much more privileged existence by comparison. We laugh about the difference quite a lot, me and Cass. I mean, whenever we are playing in Dublin, the first thing we do on arrival at the Airport Hotel is to sprint down to the room, switch on the telly, jump into bed with the sheets around our ears and wait for Mick to arrive with the Mars bars and tea. Then, as soon as he leaves the room, we'll take a sip and look at each other and go: 'Ahhh lovely innit?' But again, for the wives it's a difficult time. Although Jackie flies out here on Thursday, she and the rest of the wives will be barred from the hotel until after the game. We'll have Saturday night together, Sunday with the kids and then on Monday she will pack her things, barred again until after the Mexico game. Sometimes she wishes I worked a nine-to-five: 'We could plan things then – a night out on Fridays, a weekend away. You can never do that with football.' She's right of course, but then there's the other side as well – the pay, the glory, seeing your name up in lights. It all comes at a price.

⚽   ⚽   ⚽

Summer of '88: Now or never, sign or scram

Towards the end of my third full season at Southampton, I knew I was
starting to establish myself when I began being contacted by agents. A
man called John Mac was the most persistent. I had tossed his earliest
letters straight into the bin, but agreed to meet him one day for a chat
in March of '88.

'Would I be right in saying that you're looking to leave Southampton?' he asked.

'Well, not desperately looking to leave,' I replied, 'but I would like
to join a club that's going the other way a bit.'

Without making any false promises, he explained a little about what
he could do for me and, suitably impressed, I agreed that he could act
on my behalf. It was my first lesson in 'transfer-speak'.

Shortly after that meeting, I happened to bump into Lew Chatterley,
who had returned to the area to live after the Sunderland experience
had turned sour. 'Look,' he said, 'I was speaking to Terry Venables
recently and he seems keen on taking you to Spurs. Would you be interested?'

I said: 'Cor, course I would... jump at it.'

'Well give him a ring.'

'Give him a ring? I can't just give him a ring.'

'Course you can. I'm telling you, I've spoken to him. Now give him
a ring.'

I thanked him for the tip-off, then immediately contacted John Mac,
who was able to confirm that Venables had phoned Chris Nicholl
and asked about my availability, but hadn't been given an answer.
Encouraged, I felt it was time for me to visit the manager.

Southampton football club changed in the three seasons that followed
Lawrie McMenemy's departure. The big names that were once the
nucleus – the Shiltons, Jordans and Mills – either retired or moved
on, and the club went from being a respected force, good enough to
qualify for Europe, to a team of also-rans, perennially struggling to
avoid the relegation zone. Lawrie's departure, in my opinion, was a
major factor. While Southampton was never a Manchester United or a
Liverpool, he had this ability to sell the place to the big boys, but Chris
Nicholl – perhaps, to be fair, because of budgetary limitations – didn't
seem as gifted in this domain. The big-name players didn't sign for
Southampton any more.

My own relationship with him was up and down and suffered from a meeting we had shortly after he arrived. Explaining about the review of my contract that Lawrie had promised me before he left, I complained that, while not exactly on the breadline, I was struggling to make ends meet and could hardly afford to take my wife out for a meal. 'Well then, you'll have to live on fish and chips,' he smirked, 'won't you?' If he'd said, 'Andy, listen. I understand what you're going through, but I need to see a bit more of you before we can talk about new contracts,' I could have accepted it. But the fish-and-chips remark meant I could never really warm to him after that. My first season under his leadership went so-so: I was in and out of the side, played in twenty-five League games, came off the bench for the second half of the FA Cup semi-final against Liverpool (we lost 2–0 in extra time) then ended the year on a real high when Daniel, our first child, was born.

My second season was the best and worst of times: out for five months after breaking my leg in a pre-season friendly (ironically enough against my old club, Weymouth), I changed a lot of nappies, got to know my son, returned and played quite well. Everything was going fine until one Friday before a home game to Villa when, picking his team, Chris Nicholl decided to leave me out. Although we had been beaten 3–0 the week before, there was no way, in my opinion, that I deserved to carry the can and, absolutely enraged, I stormed into his office.

'I want you on the bench tomorrow,' he explained.

'You can stuff it up your arse,' I replied. 'I'm not sitting on any bench tomorrow – in fact, if you want me I'll be in London.'

'Well, if you do that you'll be in trouble.'

'Then so be it.' And I went AWOL.

The following afternoon, good as my word, while Southampton were running out at The Dell, I was pushing a pram around the shops in Bexleyheath with Jackie. Curiosity got the better of me at a quarter to four. I remember staring in the window of a Radio Rentals store waiting for the half-times to come up. Southampton were leading 4–0 and added one more in the second half. 'Oh shit,' I thought, because as much as I didn't want to see them lose, a 5–0 win was the worst possible result for me. The following Monday I went back with my tail between my legs and apologised. Rapped sharply on the knuckles, as I deserved to be, I buckled down and was back in the side for the rest of the season. My third season was easily my best: although still uncomfortable in the role I was being asked to fill (wide left), I was a first-team regular and was attracting interest from other clubs.

Chris Nicholl didn't surround you in the office in the way Lawrie McMenemy did. As a result, it was easier to be aggressive, easier to speak your mind. The season was winding down when I requested a meeting to clarify the rumours I had been hearing.

'I want to know what's happening. Is it true that Tottenham have come in for me?' I asked.

'No, they haven't.'

'Are you being honest with me boss?'

'Are you calling me a liar?'

'No.'

'They haven't.'

'Well I've heard different.'

'Well what you've heard is wrong, son.'

Sorely tempted to point out to him that my agent had just come off the phone with Terry Venables and had just been told different, I resisted. Transfer-speak, you see, is a very peculiar language, because managers are forbidden to contact players, or players' agents, until a transfer fee with the player's club has been agreed. 'Officially' the conversation between John Mac and Terry Venables had never taken place. So I bit my lip and said nothing.

There was no further discussion until the season ended and I headed off to St Austell in Cornwall for a few days' break with Jackie, Daniel and some friends of ours. But the rumours about Spurs and Terry Venables were persisting and I found it hard to relax. One afternoon, they got the better of me. Racing from the golf course with a handful of 50p coins, I decided I would ring the great man himself.

'Hello, Mr Venables? It's Andy Townsend here.'

'Oh hello, son, how are you?'

'I'm fine thanks... emmm, Lew Chatterley asked me to give you a call.'

'Has he? Well he shouldn't have done that.'

(Oh God.)

'Look, I'll tell you the situation, son. I've enquired about your availability and I haven't had any reply. I've asked Chris Nicholl a number of times, but he hasn't come back to me and I don't know what he is doing. Why don't you go and see him yourself and then come back to me?'

Encouraged by his interest, I decided to probe further: 'Emmm if we could work out a deal, where would you envisage playing me, Mr Venables?'

'Well, basically where you've being playing for Southampton. Have you a problem with that?'

'No... it's just I prefer to play in midfield really.'

'Couldn't you play at left back?'

'Well, not with four, no. I can play left back with five going up and down a bit, but I'm not a defender.'

'Well look, as I've said, he hasn't come back to me yet. Why don't we monitor the situation, and if you hear anything come back to me.'

Advised to let things lie until after the summer recess, we booked a holiday in June and jetted off to the Spanish island of Minorca.

On the morning of June 12, as I pulled back the curtains to another cloudless Minorcan sky, a day at the beach was the last thing on my mind. A week of sun, sea and the pleasure of my wife's company had left me thirsting for the very thing I had come here to escape – football. The European Championships were being held in Germany, and later that afternoon England were playing Ireland in their opening game. Racing down to reception, I explained as best I could in my very limited Spanish about my need to be near a TV. But our hotel – no Hilton – was in a tiny village and it was explained to me that my only chance was to make the seven-kilometre bus ride into Ciudadela.

I have never been that patient when it comes to waiting, and after fifteen minutes of standing at the bus stop, I decided that a seven-kilometre run wasn't beyond my physical threshold and would do me good. But it was hot and, without the proper running shoes, it wasn't long before the pounding of the road was exacting its toll on my legs and feet, so that my run had slowed to a jog and then to a walk. Then I noticed this bike against a wall: a bit of a heap, it seemed to have lost its owner, so I decided to 'borrow' it, as you do. An English bar seemed my best bet and after a quick lap of the town I found one. Parking the bike against the wall, when I went in I was amazed – not by the fact that it was so full in the afternoon, but that it was wall-to-wall Irish. I sat down and ordered a beer, an anonymous Englishman in a sea of green.

The game started. England looked good but then, after just seven minutes, Ray Houghton put Ireland in front. The bar erupted: 'Cooome on you boysen green, come on you boysen green, come on you boys,

come on you boys in green.' Surprised and slightly stunned by the
frenetic reaction, I thought, 'Oh.' From my earliest days, you see, I had
always been an England supporter. I remember in particular pacing the
floor in agony during the World Cup qualifier at Wembley in '73: the
Poles' one strike of the game slithering under Shilton's body; the inspired
brilliance of Tomaszewski denying England as they tried to pull one
back; the time ticking away; my brother Mike counting down the
seconds with increasing panic. It seemed like the end of the world. And
why not? We came from Kent, didn't we? Wasn't it natural for us to
want England to win?

And so it was in Minorca that day: if Bobby Robson and Jack
Charlton had both come through the door seconds after Ray's goal and
said 'your country needs you', I would have walked off happily with
Robson. That I would one day play with Ray Houghton, one day
captain Ireland in the World Cup finals, one day have these lads in the
pub cheering my name couldn't have been further from my mind.

When the game was over, one beer led to another as I joined in the
lads' celebrations, so that it was dark and after eleven before I eventually escaped. I hadn't the money for a taxi and, dismayed to discover
that 'my' bike had been stolen, I set off on foot in the darkness for the
hotel. Jackie was waiting in reception when I arrived. It was well after
midnight.

'Where on earth have you been?' she asked, concerned.

'Watching the match.'

'But the match finished six hours ago.'

I tried to explain. About the bar. And the lads. And the match. And
Ray Houghton's goal. And the crack after the game... but I'm not sure
how it came out, because deep down I was still in a state of shock.
'Jackie, you won't believe this. England lost!'

The transfer-speak resumed during pre-season training. Left out of the
friendlies after a series of heated rows, on the Tuesday before the
season was due to start I asked to see Chris Nicholl again for the latest
on the official moves.

'Look, I know for a fact that Tottenham have been on to you.'

'No, you don't know. I've had a couple of offers for you all right,
but nothing from Tottenham.'

'Are you sure? Haven't you told them whether I'm available or not?'

'They haven't asked.'

Biting my lip again: 'Well that's not what I'm hearing.'

'I've had an offer for you from Bradford which wasn't big enough...'

'Well that's okay then, because I'm not going to Bradford.'

'...and I've had an offer from Norwich.'

'I don't want to go to Norwich, I want to go to Tottenham.'

'But Tottenham haven't... I haven't agreed a fee with Tottenham. I've agreed a fee with Norwich. Now, if you want, you can go and talk to them.'

That he should have agreed to let me go gave me a bit of a jolt. It's what I wanted, it's what I had been arguing for, yet when it actually happened, it was almost a kick in the pants. I went home, phoned John Mac and he arranged a meeting with Robert Chase (the chairman) and Dave Stringer (the manager) at Norwich on Thursday. But the plot thickened considerably next day when I was contacted (unofficially of course) at home by the assistant manager of Chelsea.

'What's your situation, son?' he asked.

'Well, I'm travelling up to have talks with Norwich tomorrow.'

'Would you be interested at all in coming to play for Chelsea?'

Very enthused: 'Yeah. Yeah, I would. Very much.'

'Right, okay, that's nice to hear. Well, look, we'll leave it at that for the time being, you go and have your talks, but don't do anything until you've heard from us again.'

Twenty minutes later the phone rang again. Bobby Campbell, the manager of Chelsea, was much more forthright. 'Listen son,' he commanded in his thick scouse accent. 'You want to come to the big city – you've been playing at a small-fry club. Come and play football for a big club; come and play for us at Chelsea.'

'Well,' I replied, a little taken aback, 'I'd be delighted to, but I've already spoken to Dave Stringer [the Norwich manager] and I'm going up to have further talks with him tomorrow. I owe him that at least.'

'Okay. Well, you do that and I'll talk to you when you get back.'

The drive up was a voyage: Jackie's first impression of Carrow Road was that it was a long way from Southampton. We met John Mac at the ground, were introduced to Robert Chase and Dave Stringer and then split up, John going into Robert Chase's office to open negotiations while Jackie and I were entertained by the manager outside. Dave Stringer seemed a very easy-going fellow. He ordered some tea and quickly made us feel welcome. Although the game – the flannel process that is part and parcel of attracting any new player to a club – was only beginning, already I was starting to enjoy it. In a way, it was just like buying a new house: you're brought in, shown all the rooms and the various gadgets and subtly pressurised into signing on the dotted line.

John came out after what seemed an age and we adjourned to another room to discuss the figures. They were good – great compared to what I was earning at Southampton – but not to the extent that I immediately wanted to sign. 'John, you've done well here, but I want to speak to Terry Venables and I want to speak to Bobby Campbell and....'

'Andy,' he interrupted, 'let me tell you now, I think this is the right move for you.' But I wasn't convinced. We discussed a bit more and then Robert Chase offered to take us on a guided tour of Norwich in his Bentley. At this stage of the proceedings, however, the sights didn't interest me: what I needed more than anything else was 24 hours to think it over. Tempted, I knew I couldn't ask for it, because what I would really be asking for is 24 hours to go and negotiate with someone else. 'You do realise the offer we've put to you today won't be available tomorrow,' Robert Chase stressed. The nuance wasn't lost on me. I was beginning to understand the game: he was raising the stakes, turning the screw. It was now or never time – sign or scram.

We returned to the ground. 'Is everything okay then? Is it all done?' Dave Stringer asked cheerily. I felt like saying: 'Dave, please, give us the keys of your office. I need to phone Chelsea and Spurs.' But again, this wasn't possible, so I replied instead that I was still thinking about it and would like some privacy to talk it over with Jackie.

Guided out through the directors' box, we weighed up the options from seats looking down on the pitch. On the plus side there was the salary, the terms, and a guarantee from Dave Stringer that he would play me in my preferred position, inside left or midfield. On the minus side, the possibility that bigger clubs like Spurs (who wanted me as a left back) or Chelsea would offer a similarly attractive deal. Was a bird in the hand worth two in the bush? Yes. I agreed to sign.

The night was spent in Norwich. Dave put us up in a top-class hotel and laid on champagne and all the trimmings as a gesture in response to our decision. Before we could begin celebrating, however, there were a couple of calls to be made.

'Hello, Mum? I've just signed for Norwich.'

Disbelieving: 'You haven't.'

'Yeah. Yeah, I have.'

'Oh dear... Bobby Campbell hasn't stopped ringing all afternoon.'

'Really?'

'Yeah. Ohhh, he'll be choked, he will. And the fella from Tottenham [Ted Buxton], he rang as well wanting to know the situation.'

'Well, they've had their chance,' I explained, defending my decision. 'They could have come and sealed it up but....'

Jackie's mother Sheila and my brother Mike, an ardent Spurs supporter, were similarly unimpressed.

Sheila: 'You haven't! Norwich!'

Mike: 'Whaaat? I don't believe you. Norwich! Did nothing happen with Spurs?'

Indeed, of our two families only our dads seemed enthused that we had made the right decision.

The following day, when I returned to Southampton to see Chris Nicholl, the change in my attitude towards him surprised me. A few days earlier I had felt like jumping across his desk and grabbing him by the neck: 'Stop messing around with my life.' I now understood that he was just doing his job and that it was nothing personal – just part of the wheeling and dealing of transfer-speak.

'You've done the deal then?' he asked.

'Yeah. Yeah, I've done it.'

'Good.'

'Look, I wish you all the best and thanks for all you've done for me.'

'That's alright, son. Good luck to you.'

And we parted. Amicably. It's a funny old game....

DAY 9

TUESDAY JUNE 14:

TUTTI FRUTTI, JASON, MICK

Are we really just four days away from playing in the World Cup? It doesn't feel like it – not once you leave the training ground, that is. There is no buzz, no hype, no tingle of anticipation about the streets. And yet, somewhere out there, the World Cup is real, it's happening. But not here. Not in Orlando. Orlando is Disneyland, fantasy land, a ledge looking in at the world. And we're out on it, waiting to be called in. Us and Mickey Mouse.

It wasn't at all like this last time. In Italy there was no Shamu or Mickey or Back to the Future rides to take your mind off the game. Not only did 100 per cent of Italians know the World Cup was happening, they wanted to sing it night and day. Old pros were dusted down, dragged from retirement and sent to report from the camps of every national team – who they liked, who they didn't like – all part of the round-the-clock analysis on TV. As a result, there was no escape... or almost no escape. There was *Tutti Frutti*, of course.

Now, although Cass and I don't possess a great grasp of Italian (I don't speak any, he speaks some), we loved *Tutti Frutti*, used to watch it every night. It was a game show, and whenever one of the contestants got a question wrong, his girl had to remove an item of her clothing. Or was that a question right? I'm not sure. Anyway, to get back to where I was earlier, apart from *Tutti Frutti* there was no escape from the game. Here it's almost the exact reverse: you switch on the TV and its a toss between *Here's Lucy*, baseball or 'eyewitness' reports on the latest murder (the stabbing on Sunday night of Nicole Simpson, wife of former American football star O.J.) or crime. Perhaps on Thursday, when we fly up to New York things will change.

As days go, it was quiet enough. Training was over two sessions – a game against an American under-23 selection in the morning (we won 4–2) was followed by set-piece practice in the afternoon, while the daily diversion at lunchtime was provided courtesy of Jason McAteer.

Sitting around with the usual hour to kill, we were playing cards and Scrabble when we noticed him scribbling diligently in the corner. Someone asked: 'What are you doing Jason?'

'Rytin'.'

'Yeah... writing what?'

'Ah, justa letter to me matz.'

Suspicions were instantly raised. If he had said he was writing post-cards, no one would have paid any attention, but a letter? To his *mate*? A scouser writing a letter to his mate? No, that didn't add up. We watched. Waited. Delighted when he slipped what he had written into his locker (a fatal mistake) and left the room. Seconds later, scavengers descending on a corpse, we had it: we were not only reviewing his pro-fession of love but editing it – being less inhibited here, more explicit there – before carefully replacing it before he returned. Now the thing is, given he had actually finished, we're not sure whether he bothered to read it again before shoving it in the post. If he did, there isn't a prob-lem. If he didn't... well, there's a pretty good chance his new girlfriend will soon be his ex. Sorry matz!

Mick seemed a little bit subdued this evening. A couple of things have been getting him down of late. It started the other night in his room. Aldo had just had some treatment for his knee and there were a few of us in the room having a chat, when Aldo said: 'Hey, what about the tea and sandwiches Mick?' Now tea and sandwiches before going to bed are, it must be explained, a bit of a tradition with the squad. So Mick phoned room service, the sandwiches arrived and, giving the lad a tip, we instructed him to have the bill signed by an official of the FAI.

Everything was fine as we sipped away, until Joe Delaney (the FAI treasurer) arrived and there was a kerfuffle over who should pay: 'You get breakfast, lunch, you've had a three course bloody dinner....' Of course, he was right in one way. I mean, we weren't starving, we didn't *have* to have them, but what he didn't understand is that it's these little threads that bind the fabric; it's the little chats you might have at that time that unite us as a team. Now, Mick *does* understand and, annoyed at the pettiness, said he would pay himself. Not that money was ever the issue. As Mick put it: 'I can't believe we are out here at the World Cup finals and are being hassled over the price of tea and sandwiches.'

Tonight, Mick's problems started over dinner. Having, in his own words, 'worked his balls off all day', he had just sat down to a nice bowl of soup when Joe Delaney arrived and informed him of a snag with his accreditation that required him to go into Orlando immediately to have a photograph done. Now, given that dinner time is usually wind-up time and that, as soon as this was announced, Kev said, 'Mick, pass us your soup if you're going out,' Mick didn't believe it at first.

'No, I'm not going,' he said, deciding to take a stand.

Jack, listening, was sitting across the table. Giving us a wink, he said: 'Well, if you don't have it done, you won't go to New York, simple as that.'

But Mick was adamant: 'Well, I won't go then. I'll watch the game from me bloody room.'

'All right then, do that,' Jack said.

After the storm, there was a calm until the lads started chipping in: 'I bet you go and have this photo done, Mick. I bet you do, I bet you do.' And though he continued to insist that he wouldn't relent, we all knew he would have to in the end. It would be unthinkable – we couldn't go to New York without Mick.

Dublin

My mum sowed the seed of my international career. Three months into my first season at Norwich, we were visiting after a game one weekend when she asked if I was aware that I qualified to play for Ireland. I was, but had never really given it much thought up until then. I can remember broaching the subject with Chris Nicholl at training one day and being told: 'At international level, son, you wait until you're asked.' I forgot about it after that; still fighting to hold down my place at Southampton, I had other priorities.

My first three months at Norwich, however, prompted a revision. We were top of the First Division and I was acquitting myself well in the weekly midfield battles against the Robsons, Whelans and McMahons, growing in confidence with each game. Whereas six months previously I was happy to get a shirt and be part of the team, suddenly taking part wasn't good enough any more. I wanted to compete, to win, to have input into the team.

As the days counted down towards Christmas, I began to give serious thought to my mum's suggestion and one night decided to ring Cass. Although our paths hadn't crossed since our days at Interfico, I had kept track of his exploits – first at Gillingham, then at Millwall –

through my brother Mike, who would occasionally bump into him in a pub near Bexleyheath. Receptive to my call, he was very encouraging indeed when I told him what I was thinking: 'You'll love it. You'll play against the best players, get to travel to different countries....' Replacing the receiver, I wasn't sure. Brilliant and all as he had made it seem, the thought of pulling on a green shirt, the thought of playing football for Ireland just didn't seem... right. I talked it over with Jackie, spoke further about it to my mum and dad, then decided to take the plunge by mentioning it to Dave Stringer after training one day: 'Look, I think I qualify to play for the Republic of Ireland.'

'And would you like to do it?'

'Yeah. Yeah, I would.'

'Okay. I'll get in touch with Jack Charlton and Maurice Setters and mention your name.'

The response came in January '89. It was an away League game, ironically enough at Cass' club, Millwall. I was standing in the tunnel talking to Ian St John after our 3–2 win, when Maurice Setters approached me. 'Hello, son,' he said. 'Is it true you want to play for Ireland?'

'Yeah, I do.'

'Okay, well there's a few things that need to be done. You'll be getting a phone call over the next few days from Jack Kelly of the FAI, who will give you a list of things to do so we can check everything out. All going well, I look forward to seeing you soon.' And that was it. As he walked away, Ian St John found the idea amusing enough to make a quip about it – the first of many I would hear over the next five years.

When Jack Kelly phoned two days later, his list was long and extensive: my birth certificate, my father's birth certificate, my mother's birth certificate, my nan's birth certificate, my father's marriage certificate and my nan's marriage certificate. Believing my eligibility to be a mere formality now, I turned the list over to my mother and informed my friends and relatives. My Uncle Roy, whose recollections of Ireland and of my nan were much more vivid than my dad's, was especially pleased.

However, just when I thought it was a *fait accompli*, my mother phoned with a problem. Jack Kelly had just been on: how could we prove that the Bridgid Browne, born on January 12, 1896 in Castleisland County Kerry, and the Beatrice Browne that married Cecil

Townsend in a register office in Swindon twenty-eight years later were one and the same? I was gutted. Having just raised my expectations, to have to lower them suddenly hurt more than I could have imagined. My mum, who had been doing all the digging and had really set her mind to it, seemed just as disappointed. 'Do you know what he's just said to me, your dad? He's said: "Well I'm sure Andy won't be too disappointed if it doesn't happen now."'

'Mum,' I interrupted, 'I'd be choked.'

'You'd be choked? I'd be bloody furious!' she replied.

Luckily, it never came to that: noting some details from my mum, Jack Kelly managed to trace a copy of the original marriage certificate in Dublin, and before the end of the month, I had not only been given the green light but had been asked to join the squad for the upcoming friendly against France in Dublin.

On Sunday February 5, I met Cass at Heathrow Airport. In my twenty-five years, I had never set foot in Ireland before and was feeling just a touch uncomfortable when our flight touched down in Dublin. Technically Irish, I was never more conscious of my Englishness and my South London accent as Mick Byrne met us off the plane. After we had collected our bags, the thirty-second drive to the Airport Hotel was disappointing. I was curious to discover more about my nan's native land and was half looking forward to a drive through the city.

At the hotel, the welcome was warm and friendly, although Jack didn't say much. I didn't know an awful lot about him then. I didn't know the man; I didn't know the mind; I didn't know the mentality of what I was about to find out. And to be honest, I didn't really care. The other players and how they would take to me was my main concern. Liam Brady, Ronnie Whelan, Kevin Moran, Paul McGrath, Ray Houghton, Dave O'Leary – this was a team with a lot of stars.

My first surprise was their friendliness towards each other: all the doors along the corridor were flung open and they drifted in and out of each other's rooms, sharing the latest gossip and jokes. I had imagined it would be different: stars are not usually renowned for their graciousness towards each other, and I had imagined them locked away in their rooms until it was time to depart for the game, when the colour of the shirt would unite them for ninety minutes. But it wasn't like that at all. The atmosphere was so relaxed – it was almost as if they were away on a holiday weekend.

Still wary of the surroundings, I stuck to Cass like glue the first night; I sat beside him at the evening meal, then followed him out to the lobby and back to the room, where he dumped me and went off to play cards. I decided to make a few calls: Jackie, my mum and dad were all impatient to hear how it was going.

'Has he told you you're playing?'

'No, I don't know nothing much.'

'Has he said...?'

'Well, no, I haven't really spoken to him yet.'

'Well, who have you bloody spoken to? Hasn't anyone said anything to you yet?'

'Well....'

That first night in the room of the Airport Hotel was the first of many I would share with Cass. Curious about Jack and the way the team played, I probed him when he returned from playing cards. Now, at Norwich, we had the reputation of being a really good footballing team that played short one-touch passes in areas where other teams didn't like to play. Cass warned me, however, that Jack's philosophy was different: 'I know what you do at Norwich looks good and all that, but for God's sake don't do none of that with us.' So I looked at him and laughed, thinking he was trying to wind me up. 'What do you mean?'

'I'm serious, Andy, don't mess about with it. If you're in any danger, have any doubts, just lump it forward. And I mean that literally. Jack's a serious fella; don't fuck him about.' And as he said it, there was a look of fear in his eyes that left me in no doubt.

Charlie O'Leary handed me my kit on the afternoon of the game. There was a long- and a short-sleeved shirt: one to keep and the other to swap after the game. Slipping the short-sleeved shirt on as I prepared to leave for the game, there was no buzz, no massive rush of emotion as it landed on my shoulders. The wearing of a green shirt didn't suddenly make me Irish; my affinity towards the team, the nation and its people would be a slowly evolving thing.

Striding out to the team coach, I was feeling quite nervous. Jack had told me earlier that morning that I was playing but nothing else and I was starting to get edgy. Michel Platini's France would be a very good team, and having been warned constantly by the lads about all the things I (absolutely) shouldn't do, what I needed quickly was some positive instruction about what I should do.

The ground was a short drive away, the weather awful. I sat at the back of the coach and listened with amusement to the lyrics of the songs blaring from the speakers overhead. Jack, wearing his trademark cap and his long coat, stood up at the top of the bus as we left the hotel, then slowly began working his way down. 'The French are a very skil-ful team,' he said, as he reached my seat and sat down. 'But I want you to chase their arses off. Don't give them any space or time to pick their passes and play it around.' His instructions were short and sharp, and as I nodded my head and listened to the intensity of his tone, I quickly understood that you didn't debate with this man. If I played it his way, we would get along fine.

Dalymount Park might not have been Wembley, but the crowd could certainly roar. The boom was just beginning after the success the pre-vious summer in the European Championships and it was a good time to be involved. In the dressing-room, we stripped off and began our warm-up routines. Cass had a final word before marching out: 'Remember Andy, mess about and he'll pull you off – he's done it to bigger and better than you, so don't think he won't. But do what he says and you'll be fine.' I would have preferred it, however, if he had warned me about the anthem. We were just about to line up for it when Chris Morris saved me from looking a right prat: 'When our anthem starts, we turn and face the flag.'

'Oh, cheers, Chris.'

The game flashed by like the click of fingers. International football is another step up the ladder and I was wary of my inexperience, con-scious of the need to avoid the dreaded square ball in and around our box. A nil–nil draw, it was probably a horrible game to watch, but as I walked from the field, the quality of what had been served was the last thing on my mind. I had survived the ninety minutes, hadn't messed up. The sparkle, hopefully, would follow later.

As soon as I returned to Norwich the letters began arriving, labelled the 'English Republican Army'. When I read them at first I thought, I've had it, I'm dead. 'We know where to find you, we know where you live', one threatened. But if they knew where I lived, they'd have posted the letter direct to the house and not to the club. I dismissed these as pranks, but there were others that were more serious. One started: 'Can I put a question to you? How would you feel if…' and it went on detail-ing a list of shootings and atrocities. 'Do you realise what you've done?

You've brought shame on yourself.' I crumpled it up and threw it in the bin. Another one started: 'I was disappointed to see you playing for the Republic of Ireland last week; surely an England cap was waiting for you in the not too distant future? It strikes me as a little strange that someone who was born in Maidstone in Kent and talks with a cockney accent should....' The only conclusion I could come to was that there are some strange people out there. But there are also some warm, kind-hearted people, and overall the positive outweighed the negative. I had so many letters from Ireland, especially from County Kerry. 'How thrilled we are... we knew your nan... it's a pleasure...' and these gave me a massive lift.

My second international call-up followed a month later – a World Cup qualifier away to Hungary – and although I didn't come off the bench, it was still great to be involved. Substitute again (I replaced Frank Stapleton after 69 minutes) in the 1–0 win over Spain at Lansdowne Road in April, I finished the summer on four caps and was recalled when the campaign resumed in the autumn.

The more I travelled to Dublin, the more I felt at ease with my new identity. The Irish people were incredibly supportive: when they stopped you on the streets to wish you well, they weren't whispering, 'There's that snake who's only here because of the money' – they were genuine. I experienced an example of this on one of my earliest trips. It was a home game at Lansdowne Road, possibly against Northern Ireland, and we were being whisked through the city with a police escort when all of a sudden this ambulance, with its blue light flashing and its siren blaring, shot out from a junction just ahead of us. Expecting the ambulance to continue its trajectory, we were amazed when the driver slammed his foot on the brake to let our bus through first. Watching, Cass and I were in total hysterics, couldn't believe what we were seeing, because as we passed and looked across, the ambulance driver had this huge smile on his face and was giving us a wave. I could just imagine the poor bugger in the back, who was probably half-dead and within seconds of losing his life. Except that he's not half-dead at all, not now that he has seen us pass. No, with a miraculous new lease of life, he has jumped off his death-bed to give us a wave too.

Sometimes, when we've come in off the pitch after a particularly good result, my mind returns to that day and the smile on the driver's face, because in many ways he sums up what my Ireland years have been all about. It's nice to be able to give something in return.

DAY 10

WEDNESDAY JUNE 15:

'DO NOT ADJUST YOUR SET MUM'

At Leeds, if there was one thing Jack hated more than anything else when he was a lad, it was the cross that dipped viciously as it arrived in your box. Too low to head, too high to kick, so that the temptation always was to step back and let it bounce and – as all good defenders know – once you let it bounce you are dicing with death. He was never one to ignore his own experiences, so the focus this morning was the viciously dipping cross and the honing of our shooting from around the edge of the box. In the afternoon, we studied a video of the recent Germany-Italy game. 'There is nothing here that should desperately frighten you,' Jack announced. Then he rolled the tape and began highlighting flaws in the Italian game.

'Now,' he said, 'the keeper [names mean nothing to him]. I'm not 100 per cent sure about their keeper. He has a habit of making easy saves look incredible and when you watch it again in slow motion you wonder, 'Why didn't he catch it?' Keepers like that always worry me.

'The left back – Maldini – whilst people call him the best full back in the world, I'm not so sure. Look what happens here....' And he showed us this slow-motion clip of the ball coming into Klinsmann, who not only holds Maldini off but manages to head it on, a cardinal sin for a defender even at club level.

The points he made about Baresi were perhaps the most interesting. More than just the captain, he is very much the fulcrum of the defence, *the* man at the back. However, while his presence at the back is undoubtedly an asset, there are times when it is also a liability. The off-side trap, for example, has long been a favourite Baresi tool but, as the video of the game against Germany showed, when he rushes out, he rarely looks across to check that his team-mates are alongside. No, once he decides to play it – bang, he's gone and the others are expected to be with him. Against Germany, however, there were times when one or two were caught ball watching, and as we all know, it only takes one to play three on-side – a weakness we hope to exploit further on Saturday.

We shouldn't, however, place too much emphasis on the Italy we watched on video today. I mean, if someone had watched us being beaten by Czechoslovakia on the day before we flew out here, they would have left with a firm belief they had witnessed a poor team. But if they had watched two of the previous games, the victories over Holland (1–0) and Germany (2–0).... And so it goes for Italy. Beaten easily by Germany, come Saturday they might be a very different team. But Jack doesn't believe it. 'I'm worried about not being worried,' he said after watching them play today. 'You are a better team than them – believe me. Okay, that's it. Let's go.' And the session was closed.

Returning to the hotel mid-afternoon we – myself, John Sheridan, Cass, Kev, Aldo and Denis – decided a hair-cut might be appropriate before flying off to war (we leave for New York tomorrow).

'Why don't you start with just a brush?' I said to Kev, whose hair looks permanently tossed. 'Then you can have it washed.' He laughed, got bored waiting, and in the end went for a coffee instead. Denis, first for shaving, requested an 'Eric Cantona' special. Shez and Aldo went for conservative cuts. Cass, worried about the unmistakable fleck of grey starting to push through, wanted his thatch restored to black, and then it was my turn. 'How long will it take to have it cut short and dyed?' I asked. 'About an hour and a half,' the girl replied. I dithered. 'You wouldn't have the bottle,' Cass jeered. 'Oh sod it,' I thought. 'It will raise a few laughs.' It did that all right – and tonight, as I sit here under my half-blond mop, I'm beginning to wonder if I did the right thing. Having gone in for a *Valderrama* (the Colombian striker), I've come out with a *Val Doonican*. 'Do not adjust your set Mum – it's me, Andy.'

Apart from the laughs my new look generated, the other major high of the day was the 'lucky' dip after dinner. It started with a gift from the University of Notre Dame. 'Hope you boys do well, have a drink on us,' the gent from the university offered, handing over some base-ball caps and a wad of US dollars. Thanking him for his kindness, we wondered how to go about dividing up the prize. While an even split between twenty-four (the twenty-two players plus Mick and Charlie) seemed the most logical, we felt that something more daring to give the evening a bit of a 'lift' would have to be devised.

Ray Houghton set to work. Drawing up a list of prizes numbered 1 to 24, he then requested that we each pick a piece of paper with a number from the hat. Standing on a chair with the list of prizes in one hand and the drawn numbers in the other, he cleared his throat to announce the results. Sounding like the guy who pulls the balls from the bag in the draw for the FA Cup, he began: 'Nummmber one... John Sheridan. Your prize... eighty dollars.' There was a spontaneous round of applause; Shez, accepting his prize, announced he was well pleased. Then the room fell quiet again as we awaited number two.

'Number two... Denis Irwin... fuck all.' A cheer went up this time. Denis stood up, raised a hand in acknowledgement and took it well. Phil Babb was next – $125; Charlie O'Leary – $20; and then we arrived at 'Number nine... Ronnie Whelan... a Snickers bar.' So Ronnie went up and, with his little double chin, laughed: 'That's the last thing I needed.' So it went on: 'Number ten... Andy Townsend... one dollar' (typical), until eventually Ray arrived at number thirteen. 'Number thirteen... unlucky for some... Tony Cascarino...' and just as we were waiting to hear 'Mars bar' or a couple of cents, he said, 'Fivvve hunnndred dollars.' I can tell you, I nearly fell off my chair. And as for Cass, well, for a fellow who hadn't trained all week with a badly torn calf, he seemed suddenly and miraculously cured and danced around the room in total delight. It's a good job Jack wasn't around.

Packed my bags for the trip to New York tomorrow. As I closed the door of my locker after training this morning, I couldn't help but wonder in what state of mind we will return here next week. How will we feel? Will we trudge in the door, physically bruised and mentally scarred after the mauling by Italy on Saturday? Or will we strut back with a spring in our step, top of the group? Who knows?

He does it *his* way: images of Jack
Vilnius, June '93: The Hotel Carolina looked like a school from the outside, but inside the marble floors of the reception area gave the impression it mightn't be bad. The trouble started from the moment we checked in and were handed our key – or rather our card, for this was the 'slot type' lock where you slipped the card in, waited for the green light and then pushed. Cass' problem was that he thought the green light meant pull and when he did, the knob came off in his hand. An argument immediately ensued about who should go down to fetch someone to open our door.

'Sorry Cass, you broke it, you'll have to go down.'

'I'm not going, you go down.' Eventually a cleaning lady, who had obviously encountered this difficulty before (the door, not the fighting cockneys), let us into our room and organised a repairman. Of the two beds in the room, the one by the window furthest from the TV was clearly the shorter straw. Normally, in the race through the door, it would have been impossible for me to get past Cass' big gangly frame and I'd have pulled it. This time, however, with fatal error he chose to take a leak, and when he came out I'd switched on MTV and had my feet up in pole position.

'Oh,' he said, realising his mistake. 'Are you sure you're all right, then, in that bed?'

'Yeah,' I smiled. 'I'm fine. You don't mind, do you?'

It was later, when we returned from training, that we began to notice the smell – in the room, in the lift, everywhere. A horrible, stale, musty smell that even the open window failed to dislodge. To our amazement, it was even in the soup when we went down to dinner.

'Ah no!' Cass said. 'He's gone and done it, hasn't he?'

'Who's that?' I asked.

'The chef. He's gone and dropped his bloody cigar in the soup.'

So I tasted it and sure enough, it tasted like absolute fag ash. Cream of Benson and Hedges no doubt. It was then that someone mentioned the 'indecent proposal'. There was no escape; it was put to one and all. Which would you take – come out here and stay in this hotel and play for a Lithuanian team for a week or let someone sleep with your wife?

To a man the response was the same: 'Naah, no way, take the missus.' It was that sort of place.

'Come up to my suite at nine,' Jack ordered, emphasising the word 'suite'. He wasn't wrong; compared to our room it was an absolute palace. As soon as you walked through the door, there was a short corridor, a dressing-room, bathroom, bedroom and a lounge, where Jack was waiting with a big smile and a small scotch. He had invited us up, not to discuss the match or the weaknesses of the Lithuanian back four, but for a game of Trivial Pursuit, the general knowledge board game. The teams were myself, Kev, Cass, John Sheridan and little Charlie (O'Leary) against Jack, Maurice Setters, Maurice Price and Joe McGrath.

The game started. The rules were that both teams could only answer through their spokesman: Jack for them, Kevin for us. I don't think I have ever played the game in a more hostile or aggressive atmosphere than in the two hours that followed. Five cheeses each: they needed to land on blue for Geography, we needed to land on brown for Art and Literature. They threw, got the five they needed and moved to Geography. 'Yesss.' Picking the card from the box, I read the question: 'In which city in the world is Portuguese most widely spoken?'

Jack looked me straight in the eye: 'Rio dee Janeiro.'

'No Jack,' I replied (admittedly quite delighted). 'It's Sao Paulo.'

'And Sao Paulo,' he countered. 'I was just about to say Sao Paulo. Bloody 'ell... I was mulling it around in my head – just about to say it, and now you've gone and given me the answer.'

Listening, we couldn't believe it, were doubled over at his outrageous cheek, but still he went on, determined to have his sixth cheese, so in the end we relented and gave him another stab.

'Okay, here you go. Geography again. Which city is known as "little Paris"?'

They thought about it. Joe and Maurice suggested Rome and The Hague, but were instantly dismissed by Jack as he racked his brain for the answer. Then, out of the blue, this alien voice said 'Brussels'. We looked across to Mick Byrne, who had been sitting all evening with his mouth closed, a supposedly neutral observer.

Jack said: 'Brussels! Nah, the Belgians 'ate the bloody French. The last thing they'd call a city is little Paris.'

Mick immediately went on the defensive, sorry he had opened his mouth: 'Well, I mean, I don't know. I'm only offering an opinion.'

But Mick was right and Kev, who knew it, immediately started to warn him off: 'Are you playing Mick or what? Because if you're not, then piss off.'

Kev's alarm only served to alert Jack who, opting for 'Brussels', gained the team their sixth cheese. Mick, of course, was sitting there all chuffed with himself, with an 'I told you so' expression that further irritated Jack. 'Look Mick, if you're playing, then sit down and play, but if you're not, then shut your bloody gob.'

The game proceeded. We drew level; six cheeses each – but they were first back to the centre of the board. We decided to hit them with History. 'Who was the sixteenth President of the USA?' Suddenly, within sight of first prize, they were stumped. Lyndon B. Johnson? Nixon? Ford? Carter? They went through them all, unable to choose. 'I think it's Abe Lincoln,' Mick chipped, but again his suggestion was greeted with scepticism from Jack.

'Abe Lincoln! Do you know what you're on about Mick? He said the *sixteenth* president! Lincoln wasn't around at that time. Come on, think about it, don't just throw out the first name that comes into your head.'

Now, again Mick was right, but firmly rebuked, his head sank below his shoulder blades and he retreated into silence. The pressure was on now. Jack thought it might be Kennedy but wasn't sure and, perhaps for the first time of the night, needed to look to Maurice Price and Joe McGrath for help. Noticing their discomfort in the spotlight, we turned the screw: 'Go on, Joe, have the balls to say who you think it is, don't just leave it all to Jack.' But Joe was playing safe, wouldn't be drawn: 'Well, no. I actually agree with Jack.'

They opted for Kennedy – a mistake which cost them the game. Jack was grudging, ungracious, furious in defeat. The slip-up had highlighed weaknesses in his team, which he immediately raced to exploit. One by one he grilled them; put them through the mill. 'What a crap team I've got here. Did you answer one question? Did you answer one single question all night?' He was still fuming as we headed off to bed. He likes to win. It showed.

Orlando, June '94: Jack didn't say that much in February of '89 when we first met in Dublin – was probably standing back, sizing me up. He's a first impressions person, you see. He either takes to you or he doesn't, and I suppose the fact that he took to me made it easy for me to like him. I remember him asking me to buy him a cap on one of my first internationals in Dublin. We were heading into Grafton Street for a bit of a stroll around, when he said: 'Do us a favour Andy. I've left me cap at home [he always wears his cap on match days]. Get us a cap in town.' He told me the size and I went in and came across this one with a check pattern in the style he usually wore. Cass said it would do all right, so I brought it back – and he was well pleased until I told him I'd spent thirteen quid.

'What! You're joking. You're taking the piss. I only ever spend a fiver on me caps.'

'Well that cost thirteen quid, Jack – straight up.'

'Receipt,' he said, holding out his hand. And when I told him I hadn't got one, he said, 'No receipt, no pay,' at which point I wanted to add, 'No cap,' but he had it in his hands and I didn't have the balls. I reminded him about it this morning on the way to the training ground:

'Jack, you do realise you still owe me thirteen quid for a cap, don't you?' And he said, 'I'll give you fifteen dollars,' breaking into a grin.

Former members of the squad have, over the years, been critical of some of his decisions, but even though a manager can't please everybody, I don't think any of them would dislike him. Not a 'big leather chair' manager, where you knock on the door, 'Come in' and he swivels around, he is very down to earth. If he has something to say to you, he'll say it. With Jack, what you see, basically, is what you get.

I had never met him at all before that first meeting in Dublin. As I was too young (three) to remember when he won the World Cup with England, my earliest memory of his playing days was the 1970 Cup final between Leeds and Chelsea that went to a replay at Old Trafford. A fanatical Chelsea supporter, I was well pleased to see him beaten that night. I think he might even have scored.

He was always big on ITV. There were the fishing programmes and that classic clip from one of his football coaching shows that would always be shown on *It'll be Alright on the Night*.

'That's it son,' he shouts to one of the kids. 'Now take it down the wing and when you get down there, whip it back across as hard as you can.' So the kid, following every instruction, races to the line, turns, crosses it low and hard... and hits Jack smack in the bollocks, doubling him over. Cue the bad language bleeper.

The first thing that impressed me about him when I joined the squad was his sense of humour. He's got a wonderful ability to be comical without trying. We might be heading towards the training ground on the bus and, starting from the top, he would work his way down. 'Good morning, Cass. You look dreadful this morning. How many pints did you have last night?' Kevin Sheedy was a regular victim. 'All right Kevin? What a nightmare you're having. I saw you playing the other week – you were awful.' Or, a few days ago, when it was absolutely sweltering and we were about to go out and sweat our arses off at the training ground, he rubbed his hands together and said: 'Ah, lovely. This is just what I want.' Then a few minutes later he'd changed his mind: 'Where's that Alan McLoughlin? But for that silly little prat, I'd be sitting on the river bank somewhere with a rod in one hand and a cup of tea in the other. Where is the little ba....'

But there is another side to him as well, a side I first recognised in

Cass' eyes that first night in Dublin. When it comes to work, you don't mess with him. With Jack, there are no grey areas, no in-between ground. His is a black and white world, and though others might argue differently, he does it his way – which is the great strength of his teams. When he took over in 1986, it took a brave man to come in and tell players of the calibre of Brady and Lawrenson: 'No, the way you are playing it is wrong. I want you to do it like this.'

It might easily have gone wrong for him. Indeed, had Ireland not qualified for Euro '88, who's to say things would have developed as they have today. But he believed in what he was doing. He still does. Over the next few days he will retreat into himself, become quieter, moodier, as he focuses on the game. He would love to see us go further than last time in Italy. He likes to win. It shows.

On the day he made me captain, I wasn't sure I wanted the job. He approached me in training on the day before a friendly international against Wales in February of '92 and said, 'Mick's knackered now, so I'd like you to do it. You've been with me long enough to know what it's all about.'

Surprised, I replied: 'Yeah, great. I'd love to, but what about Paul [McGrath] and Kev?'

'Well, you know Paul, he'd rather not. And I'm looking for someone a bit more long-term than Kevin, someone to take us through to the World Cup. Look, don't worry about it; I'm not asking you to be or play anything different. All you've got to do is walk out first – you might have to say the odd word now and again, but if you don't like it, or can't do it, we'll change it.'

So I accepted, with reservations – so many reservations that I felt like knocking on his door that night and telling him I couldn't do it. Although I was captain of Chelsea at the time, I felt... I don't know, I just didn't feel it was right for me to be captain of an Ireland team with Kevin and Paul and so many big home-grown lads around. The fact that it would leave us even more wide open to the old mercenary rubbish wasn't lost on me either: 'Hey, look, even the captain talks with a cockney accent.' But I decided to give it a go.

In the two years since, my relationship with Jack hasn't changed; there is no special manager-captain bond between us. I'm much happier being one of the lads and I think he understands it's the way I prefer to be. While it is a great honour to be captain, there are elements of it that I don't particularly enjoy. I don't enjoy having to stand up at functions and make speeches.

Just before we came away, when Guinness hosted this big reception in London with Albert Reynolds there, Jack came up to me and said: 'Right, go on. You're going to have to introduce him to all the players – and don't forget his wife.' Panicking I said: 'Well what shall I call him – Taoiseach?'

'Nah,' Jack laughed. 'Call him Albert like me.'

And I laughed: 'I can't....'

He's popular. Very popular. The Irish people have really taken him to their hearts. In trying to reason this out, one incident springs to mind. It was during the last World Cup, the Holland-Germany game when Frank Rijkaard and Rudi Voller had a go at each other and Rijkaard spat. Now Jack was in a studio somewhere, analysing the game for ITV, and when it was over he was asked, 'What about that Jack? What would you have done if Rijkaard had done that to you?' Jack said, 'I'd 'ave chinned him,' making no attempt to be diplomatic at all. Can you imagine Graham Taylor in a similar situation? He'd have taken a quarter of an hour... 'Well, obviously these are the sort of things that happen at international level and you've just got to bite your tongue.'

But not Jack. 'I'd 'ave chinned him.' And he said it like he meant it. As I watched, my mind flashed to what the people who were watching back in England and in Ireland would think of him. 'Quite right,' they were saying in their millions. 'I'd have done the same.'

DAY 11

THURSDAY JUNE 16:

A MESSAGE FOR SONNY, JACKIE AND ITALY

The flight to New York was relatively hassle-free, apart from the 06:30 wake-up call – Mick had his work cut out this morning, I can tell you. A police escort, waiting with the bus on the Tarmac at Newark airport, guided us directly to the Tara Sheraton, where we were ambushed by a fresh batch of press and photographers as we entered the lobby. An Italian TV crew asked for my impressions on the game – or rather the team.

What do you think of Arrigo Sacchi's tactics?

'Well, he does have his critics in Italy, but to be fair....'

How do you think Italy will play?

'I think Italy are and always have been a class....'

'Do you think Italy can win the World Cup?'

'Well I think....'

As the questions dragged on, it became increasingly obvious to me that there was just one team on the reporter's agenda, but then, just when I was beginning to despair, he produced a classic. 'Have you,' he asked, 'a message for the Italian people?' Now, the last time a reporter asked a footballer a question of that nature, it made headlines across Europe. The reporter, if you will allow me to jog your memory here, was Norwegian. The footballer – Paul Gascoigne. The interview took place shortly before the World Cup qualifying game between England and Norway and, when asked if he had 'a message for the Norwegian people', Gazza replied: 'Yes, fuck off Norway.'

Okay, so it was an outrageous thing to say. But to be fair to Gazza, he is a funny lad and, given the way this prat had been grilling me for the last ten minutes – 'What do you think of Baggio, is he the best player in the world?' – I could almost understand how he would have been driven to it as I contemplated how I'd reply. 'Have I... [it's on the tip of my tongue]... a message for... [begging to jump out]... the Italian people?' (I shouldn't.) 'Well, yes, actually I have... [I shouldn't]... *arrivederci*.' (I don't). I think that means goodbye.

Tonight, after more than a week of the bliss of single rooms, we are reunited with our 'partners': Kevin is back with Paul, Stan with Ronnie, Ray with Aldo, Denis with Roy and as for me, I'm back with my old mate Cass. Ten days of solitary confinement hasn't changed him: within minutes, our 200-dollars-a-night luxury suite had been transformed into a tip. He's off playing cards at the moment: bath half-empty, clothes scattered at random around the floor, and from the tangled linen that was once a bed, you'd swear he'd spent the afternoon with Sharon Stone. Having said that, for all his untidiness (I'm completely innocent, you understand), I do enjoy his company, and it's appropriate we're together again before the first game, because it was Cass who first informed me we had drawn Italy back in December. I remember his reaction. Having spent the day watching Villa get beaten at Old Trafford (I was injured), I had completely forgotten it was on until he phoned, just after nine.

'Did you hear? Did you hear?' he asked.

'No, who've we got?'

'Italy.' And as he said it, he groaned.

The interesting thing about this groan is that it wasn't so much disappointment at the severity of the draw as the memory of what had happened last time we played Italy in Rome. As nightmares go, it started innocently enough: two days before the game, we had spent the morning training and returned to the hotel, where there was a pile of messages for Cass shoved under the door.

'A Mr Michael Cascarino called and says he will call back later.'

'A Mr Luigi Cascarino phoned this morning – says he will call back.'

'A Mr Sonny Cascarino called this morning, will try again this afternoon.'

Now, although I was aware of the fact that his grandparents were native Italian, as soon as he read out the names I was sure this was some kind of joke. But he wouldn't hear of it; swore he knew them one and all. 'This one,' he said, showing me one of the slips of paper, 'he comes from my father's side....'

We showered and changed, and later that afternoon the Cascarino clan were all as good as their word: 'Can their long-lost cousin secure them a ticket for the match?' Of course he can – at a price. Fifteen hundred dollars he spent on tickets for the game for uncles and cousins. 'See you back here when it's over,' they told him, delighted. 'We'll pay you for the tickets then.' Only they didn't, did they? No, once the game was over, Sonny and Michael and Luigi were all off to Naples (for the semi-final) with the boys in blue, leaving Cass at a loss for words. And lira. Which brings us back to the groan. He's expecting to hear from them again any day now…. I might just leave a note for him tomorrow under the door.

My wife has gone missing somewhere in New York. So has Stan's (girlfriend) and Cass'. They're together. We think. We've being trying to contact them all night. I've just left a message on the answering machine at their hotel: '*Is there any danger at all that one of you might think of giving us a call?*' Which is really most unlike me. Normally it's the other way around.

 **DAY 12**

FRIDAY JUNE 17:

'O.J. SIMPSON IS IN THE CAR'

When Jackie called this morning, I gave her a right taste of my mind: 'What the bloody hell do you think you are doing? As if I haven't got enough to worry about with the game against Italy tomorrow, you go missing in New York!' Now this, I must admit, was more than a little rich, (a) because the boot has been on the other foot loads of times when I've been away and not phoned home, and (b) because I'm not really worried about the game at all – in fact I'm really looking forward to it. But I couldn't tell Jackie that, could I? Had to ram my frustration home and, as a result, the conversation was brief and rather crusty. As I broke off to go training, she said she would come to the hotel later to collect her tickets for the game.

The Giants Stadium was impressive to say the least. The Italians, who had been given first bite, were still out on the pitch when we arrived. 'I'm sorry, you'll have to wait,' an American official insisted, as we stepped off the bus to join them. But waiting was a problem. We were eager now. After months of incessant interviews, weeks of intensive training and eleven days out on a ledge with Mickey Mouse, we could smell it. It was here in the Giants Stadium, waiting for us on the other side of this tunnel: Ireland v Italy. Game number four of the World Cup finals.

'Ah hell, lads. Come on, let's just walk out.'

For the second time we were stopped. 'You must wait until the last of their players is back in the dressing-room,' the official insisted, as if it was going to take something from the game if the teams saw each other before kick-off. We waited. The Italians were shepherded in and we were at last given the green light to walk out on the pitch.

A condensed version of Wembley, with a bowl rather than an oval shape, it almost seemed too small to house a football pitch. But when you stood at the centre circle, the view was impressive – so impressive that as I stretched and warmed up, I found it difficult to stop myself looking around. My eyes were everywhere. Then Jack called us together to announce the eleven who would start next day. This, in hindsight, was a pretty tense moment. As I was sure of my own selection, it didn't strike me at the time but tonight, looking back, there were undoubtedly a couple of tight stomachs and crossed fingers as we gathered to hear the team. He started: 'Packie... Denis Irwin... Paul McGrath... Jason...' then corrected himself, '...sorry, Phil Babb... Terry Phelan... Ray Houghton... Roy Keane... John Sheridan... Andy Townsend... Steve Staunton and Tommy up front.' Then, after naming the team, he announced the plan for the session: 'I want a quarter of an hour each way [from those who are playing]. The rest of you, put the bibs on and just get a feel of the ground for now.'

I was very pleased for Ray, who had been left out and messed around a bit during the season at Villa – it was only towards the end when he got back in the team for a few games that he had the chance to show what he could do. I hope he plays well tomorrow. Jason, who must have run him close in the race for the nod, is a young kid with an enormous future ahead of him and his time will undoubtedly come – it might even come before the tournament is out, who knows – but for a game like tomorrow's, I'm glad Jack went for Ray's experience instead. He knows the game, has been really putting it in of late, and when he's playing well and the team are playing well, he's an important link in the chain. But I'm also pleased for him personally: people are always so quick to jump on the bandwagon, but Ray is far from over the top. I hope tomorrow he goes out and answers them all with a performance.

Training over, the rest of the day passed quickly enough. I watched Germany-Bolivia (the opening game of the tournament) in the afternoon, talked a little about Italy with Jack on a live-link we did with ITV and, after Jackie had called for her tickets, spent the rest of the evening watching the latest leg of the basketball finals between the Knicks and Rockets with Cass in the room.

Or at least, that's what we set out to watch, but the game had only just started when it was suddenly interrupted by a news flash and helicopter images of a fugitive in a white car being chased by a convoy of police along some highway in California. We switched – once, twice, three times – but six different channels were showing the same pictures. Well, similar pictures, for the camera angles were different – which in some ways was the most amazing thing of all. I looked at Cass: 'How many choppers have they got up there with this guy?' Then Ronnie came crashing through the door. 'Have you seen what's on the telly?' he gasped.

'Yeah, ridiculous isn't it?'

And it was. I mean, if you didn't know better and had just tuned in, you'd have sworn you were watching *CHIPS* (*California Highway Patrol*). But this was live. For real. The message plastered on the bottom of the screen told us so. It said: 'O.J. Simpson is in the white car.'

Although he is one of American football's all-time greats, I must admit I had never heard of O.J. Simpson before the start of the week. Since Monday, however, after his former wife, Nicole, and her acquaintance, Ron Goldman, had been savagely stabbed to death, the news bulletins have led with little else. On Monday he was being 'questioned'. On Thursday, attending the funeral with his kids. Today, at lunchtime, he had sensationally become a fugitive, just as he was about to be arrested and charged by police. And this evening, the fugitive was live on our screens, being chased across Los Angeles by half the state police.

Watching, we couldn't believe it. I mean, this is the equivalent of a Keegan or a Dalglish we're talking about here! Picture it as it unfolded before our eyes. The white Ford Bronco is speeding up the motorway, O.J. Simpson is crouched in the back with a gun to his head, fifteen police patrol cars behind are giving chase... and yet not giving chase, because they know exactly where he's going – he told them in the suicide note they found when they went to make the arrest. He's going to his mum's, is being driven to his mum's by a friend, so they follow – but don't really chase, because the friend... he's told them about the gun, and not to get close, and how he just wants to go and talk to his Mum.... The roadsides are starting to crowd now... people have been watching TV, know he is coming their way. They're cheering him – 'Go O.J.' 'Free the juice' – cheering the man accused of slicing his former wife's throat. The Ford Bronco moves on... some of his friends, former greats from the football field, appeal to him over the air (radio): 'O.J. if you can hear me, man, pull over and give yourself up. This isn't the way to do it.' But O.J.'s not listening. The white Bronco moves on to his mother's house.... Soon the final scene. Once inside the drive, the car pulls up, the police cautiously maintain distance, the friend is clearly pleading with them now to let O.J. leave the car to speak to his mum, but the police don't want to know. The fugitive is armed, dangerous. Who knows where he would turn with his feet on the pavement? Stalemate. Ten minutes pass... it's getting dark. Temporary lights are brought in. Every TV in America is tuned to this little street, waiting for the bullet, for the *boom*, for the car to shake, then shudder. Waiting for the commentator to say, 'Oh my God, he's shot himself, he's done it'... only it doesn't happen. He puts down the gun and hands himself over – suddenly. Like all of America, you feel strangely disappointed, hugely let down. You've forgotten that what you've being watching has been live TV, not the latest Harrison Ford from the video store.

Mick arrives with a 'sleeper', but I'm not sure I'll need one tonight. Sleep has always come easily to me on the night before a game; I do not 'think' about football. I'm not one for lying in bed until the small hours of the morning, visualising the winning goal or worrying about the mistake that might cost us the game. It's not that I'm an 'ice-man' or anything macho like that, it's just the way I am. Funnily enough, the last time I had trouble sleeping was exactly this time four years ago, when a mosquito with a taste for RH positive pitched his buzz in my room for the night. With our opening game against England in Cagliari next day, I couldn't afford not to sleep, but as soon as I shut my eyes, the bastard set to work, 'mmbizzzz'. I tried everything to get some peace: shut my eyes, put a pillow over my head, thrashed about with a towel for ten minutes, trying to nail him to the wall, but it was no good, and the following morning when I went down for breakfast, the strain was clear to see. 'Good God, you look shit!' one of the lads laughed. 'Worried about the game?' I wasn't. I'm not.

DAY 13

SATURDAY JUNE 18:

WE COME TO BURY SACCHI

10:00 Because of the afternoon kick-off, there is no official wake-up call. I wake just before ten, stroll down to breakfast – tea, scrambled egg, toast. Not too many of the players around. Jack's there. He seems nervous, tense, not outwardly trembling or anything like that, but I can sense it. It's a big day for a manager. You've been building for it, waiting for it for so long, until finally the day arrives – and all you want to do is get it out of the way.

11:00 For as long as I've been with the squad we've walked on the day of a game. We stroll out, note the warm, muggy heat and walk what is basically a lap of the hotel grounds before returning to gather around this huge conference table for the final team talk.

Jack's tune has slightly changed. All this week he has been nonchalant about the Italians: 'Don't worry too much about them; they're not supermen.' Now it's: 'If you let them do this or let them do that, they'll skin you. Baggio… Baggio has to be watched at all times. Free kicks… don't turn your backs on any dead-ball situation… touch them and they'll not only go down but roll over… don't backchat the referee.'

In fairness to Jack, our attitude has changed as well. Whereas earlier in the week there would always be an element of eyes-on-your-feet, wishing you were some place else, this time everyone is really tuned to what he is saying, hooked on his every word. 'Get at them,' he finishes. 'Chase them. Chase their arses off and you'll get chances. Okay, that'll do. Come on.'

12:00 Cass and I return to our room, flop on to our beds and watch the golf (the US Open) for an hour and a half. While all the things we have done this morning are routine for the day of a game, there is something quite different about the attitude among the players; everyone seems confident, relaxed, there are no bad vibes. In Italy, the build-up seemed a lot more tense. Does it get easier second time around? Is the recent success against Holland and Germany a factor? Has the indifference of the hosts and the absence of 24-hours-a-day replays of Baggio's greatest hits contributed to how good we feel four hours before the game? I don't know. I wonder what Baggio and Baresi and Donadoni are thinking now. Have they spent the morning talking about us? Is Roberto flaked out on his hotel bed at this moment watching Ernie Els? Hmmm. 'Oooh nice putt. Well done, mate.'

13:30   The lobby is packed as we make our way to the bus: supporters looking for autographs, photographs. I avoid eye contact, keep my head down, keep walking. This isn't the time or place. I just want to get on the bus... sit at the back... stare out the window. Charlie shoves in the cassette. We leave the car park, turn right for the highway. In front, the card school split a deck. Something's not right with the engine as we begin to pick up speed. It's the gears – they change up and then down again, up and down. Smiling to myself, I can picture what is about to happen: the plume of thick smoke, the slow crawl to the hard shoulder, the players filing out one by one to stick out their thumbs, and Jack at the top of the line – he's got the cardboard and the marker, holding it up as the cars fly by – 'Giants Stadium please'. Thankfully it doesn't come to that; the gear box holds together.

14:15   The Italians have beaten us to it again, and as we arrive at the stadium one or two are already pacing up and down outside their dressing-room door. 'Right,' says Jack as we step inside ours. 'There will be no warming up on the pitch today – there's an official opening ceremony starting at ten past three. Now, if you want to go for a walk, you can walk around under here, but I'm not having anyone running up and down outside. You don't need it.' Jack pricks his ears up at the scale and suddenness of the departure following the licence to walk: 'Where have they all gone? Have they all gone out? Bet they're out there. Bet they've all gone out on the fucking pitch.' I follow him as he sets out in pursuit towards the tunnel – too late. They are already standing in the middle of the pitch.

'How many do you think we'll have?' I asked Kevin, just before the coach had arrived at the ground.

'Loads,' he said. 'I bet we'll have loads.'

'But we're going to be outnumbered?' I suggested. 'We're going to be swamped?'

'Oh, I wouldn't be so sure,' he wisely replied.

How right he was. As I follow Jack out on to the pitch, I can't get over how many Irish are already in their seats. 'I thought our allocation was 6,000 or something. Where on earth did they get all these tickets?' The stadium, impressive when empty the day before, is really looking special, but after five minutes of standing and staring, Jack decides enough is enough: 'Okay, that's it. Off. Everybody in.'

14:45 Packie decides it is time to begin as soon as we return inside. Slap, slap, slap go his palms off his knees as he bounces up and down off his toes. 'Crikey, Pat, you're starting a bit early. You're going to have to go through it all over again,' I think to myself, looking at my watch. Elsewhere around the room, some of the others are not nearly as anxious. Kev asks Mick if he has brought the cards from the bus, then joins Cass, Denis and Shez for a quiet game in the corner. Jack prowls the room, armed with a bottle of water: 'Drink,' he orders. 'Flood yourself with the stuff.' I comply, then take a leak and then another leak. For the next half hour my life is a shuttle run to the toilet.

15:20 *'Forty minutes to kick-off.'* Every few minutes the room shakes with the latest reminder. With half an hour to go, I decide to kick-start my own routine. Charlie gives me a T-shirt. I put it on, reach for my shorts and begin a series of stretches. The room is starting to buzz now; the talk is boots – studs or rubbers. A FIFA official knocks on the door and requests to speak to the captain.

'Hodanovitch yabela yholar chlarzdabek,' (or something like that) he begins, then pauses to allow his message to be translated from his native Russian. 'FIFA would like to congratulate Ireland on their marvellous achievement in qualifying for World Cup USA '94 and I thank you.'

'Well, that's very nice of you, thank you.'

'Yiplee galsnot-ot ovitch.... You as team captain must stress upon your players not to retaliate, not to cause any situation that may provoke the crowd.'

'Right, okay.'

'Maldinovaitasovitch bretzsky.... But we think especially the Irish team have no problem with this.'

'Fine.'

'Halgladinovanitchka.... If your team scores a goal, please keep your celebrations low key.'

'Will do, okay.'

We shake hands. He leaves the room.

15:45 *'Fifteen minutes to kick-off,'* reminds the talking clock. It's time for the final act and I remove the T-shirt I've worn to stretch and warm up. Boots polished, socks and shorts and shin-guards in place, I slip my jersey over my shoulders and Mick hands me the arm band. An official pops his head around the door: 'Okay, gentlemen, we're ready.' And with this a huge roar goes up, *'Come onnn,'* as we circle the dressing-room, slapping each other down the shoulder, wishing each other the best and shaking hands. I make for the door at the head of the string. Jack, who hasn't really said that much, is waiting with a final word.

'Good luck, Andy. Good luck, son. All the best.'

'Cheers, Jack.'

We're ready now. I turn with a final chant, 'Let's go for it lads,' and step out. A FIFA official, waiting outside in the corridor, approaches to guide us towards the tunnel, but as soon as he sees our strip, a look of horror comes over his face. 'You can't walk out there dressed in white [socks], green [shorts] and white [shirts] – Italy have just gone out wearing white, blue and white. You'll have to change.'

At first I think he's joking. 'Can we not just change the shirts,' I ask, 'and wear white [socks]-green-green?'

'No, the socks… everything must be changed.'

16:00 Pandemonium in the dressing-room. After one and a half hours of sitting twiddling our thumbs, we've got one and a half minutes to strip and change our kit. Charlie, our kit man, literally dives into the skip, emptying it furiously – shirts, socks and shorts flying around the room.

'Twenty-one? Who's twenty-one?'

'Yeah, over here.'

'Thirteen?'

'Who's got my shorts, anyone seen an eight?'

'Mine's a seven, Charlie.'

The scene of manic chaos is just too much for Jack. Turning his rage on Charlie, he completely blows a fuse: *'What the fucking hell is going on? What are we doing in the wrong kit?'* Not that it's poor Charlie's fault (I fear he might suffer a heart attack) – he never gets his kit wrong, was only doing what he was told. Socks up, boots laced, inquest put on hold, we quick-march out the door.

16:03   Just like the time we met the boys from Rollins College, face to face with our adversary for the first time, we look them up and down. You have to hand it to the Italians – they have nothing if not style. Baggio is there, looking cool and immaculate in his white-blue-white. Not to mention his tan and his ponytail and... set of matching boots. Blue boots! I can't believe it, but scanning the feet of his team-mates, I see they are wearing the same. As I take my place alongside Baresi, a man with a walkie-talkie immediately leads us on to the field. Noise and heat are the first impressions. The noise, deafening in its intensity, is welcomed. Incredibly, as I gaze around the ground, I see that the majority of the flags and banners are ours. The heat, on the other hand, is more daunting. 'Good God, this is going to be tough,' I remind myself.

16:05   Lining up for the protocol, we scan for the position of the flag to face during the playing of our anthem. For some strange reason, however, there doesn't seem to be one today. The Italian anthem is played. A section of their support, standing directly in front of us, are suddenly fired. 'It-al-ia, It-al-ia.' Glancing towards their line, I'm curious to see if any of their players are bellowing the anthem out. They don't seem to be. Baresi certainly isn't. Then it's our turn. As the first bars ring out, I notice the TV camera starting to zoom in on me as it begins its passage down our line. Should I move my lips and sing the two or three lines I know? I'd like to, but, I don't feel confident enough, and it doesn't feel right to pretend. People often send me the words, and I understand why they would like me to sing it, but the truth is I'm not sure even if many of the home-grown lads can sing it. Is Packie singing it now? I'm not sure – hard to make out. Everyone is so out of time that it's at four different stages around the ground. It ends. Then ends again. A deafening roar from our support goes up. The lads sprint off. The ref calls Baresi and me in. We exchange pennants, toss a coin – lucky side up. I decide to opt for the ball.

16:10   Kick-off: ahhh. The first five minutes are hell. My body is performing like the bus on the way to the ground – legs leaden, heart racing, lungs heaving – and the harder I try to shift up, the more it wants to shift down. A second wind arrives and the second five are easier. Cat and mouse, probe and test time, they tease us with the ball, trying to keep hold of it. Despatched to midfield for the attention of Albertini, it is returned to Baresi who, with time, casually feeds Maldini. In and out, up and down, I can almost hear their manager and what he was saying to them before the game: 'Keep the ball. Make them run. Don't worry, you won't have to wait. They'll come to you. They'll chase. But don't let them get there. Play it fast. Keep it moving. Knacker them out. That's the way to beat this team.'

16:21   Our turn now. Denis Irwin pumps a ball into Tommy Coyne but Costacurta gets there first and then Baresi, whose weak headed clearance lands neatly on Ray Houghton's chest. Transferring the ball to his feet, Ray sets off diagonally across the pitch. Stan, facing him, out wide to the left, is the obvious ball. He's thinking, 'Give it to me Ray, give it to me Ray,' and Ray is just about to let it go – 'Okay Stan here it comes' – because Tassotti, the left back, is about to close him down. But then Tassotti changes his mind. Reading the move, he cuts out Ray's option and runs to Stan… except that Ray hasn't released yet. He has the ball. He is the danger and, checking his run directly opposite their goal – 'Sod it, why not?' – he swivels and shoots… only he hasn't so much picked his spot as swung his left and weakest foot at it. The ball sails skyward. Pagliuca raises a hand but not his feet, expecting it to sail over the bar – and it would have if at that moment he had been standing on his goal-line. But he wasn't, was he? Already beginning to drift as it passed his outstretched fingertips, the ball dips and tumbles exhausted into the net. The stadium erupts. Ray's got his arm in the air, sprints toward the bench, tumbles onto the grass… is covered in ecstatic green shirts. 'He's scored! Ray's scored!' Racing to join the celebrations, I notice the contrasting scenes beyond the touchline. Our bench are up on their feet, out on the pitch, jumping up and down with joy. A couple of feet away, though, the Italians are still. Silent, stunned.

16:22   Jack, as always, is the first to get his feet back on the ground. 'Water, water, take some water,' he screams. We take a quick gulp and run back out, delighted with what is an absolutely dream start. Scoring first in this game was always going to be the most important. Forced immediately to raise the tempo, holding and waiting no longer good enough for them, Italy are behind and suddenly chasing the game.

We settle. They bicker. Baresi is on the ball. With plenty of time, he runs out to our blanket across the midfield. Decision time – he lifts his head and looks for the obvious move, the simple pass, but it's not on. He swears. It frustrates him. He runs back to Costacurta who plays in to Donadoni who plays it back to Tassotti. In and out, up and back, just as it was in the first ten minutes, except that holding is no longer good enough – they need to cut us open, slice us apart, but first they must find the knife, the probing ball. It's not happening. Donadoni and Evani are out of it in midfield and instead the better chances fall to us. Stan whips a great cross towards me in the box, but my first touch is poor and the ball drops behind me. I spin and try to connect with my weaker right. Pagliuca easily saves.

16:55 The cold blast of the air conditioning slaps you as you walk off the pitch. Half-time. One-nil. Around the dressing-room there is absolute delight, but the price we have paid is written on everyone's face. Cass runs over: 'If you keep making those runs, you're gonna die, you're not going to get through the game. We're 1–0 up, you've got to slow it down.' He's right – but rest comes first. My shirt is sodden. I take it off, lie on the floor, put my feet on a chair and slap an ice-towel over my steaming face and neck. I feel knackered, so knackered it worries me. I say to Mick: 'Mick, I can't believe this, I don't think I'm gonna get through this okay.' He hands me a bottle, tells me I'm great and that everything will be okay.

Jack is pleased: 'Well done, you've done ever so well, keep chasing for forty-five minutes. They're getting frustrated, running out of ideas. Keep doing what you are doing.' The fifteen minutes pass quickly. Time to return to battle. We wait for a fresh shirt, a dry pair of shorts – but we've forgotten the problem with the kit. Having packed a double set of white, Charlie never for one minute expected we'd be running out in green. We take the shirts, wring them out, slip them on. If you've ever had occasion to use wet swimming trunks at the beach, you'll know a little how that feels.

17:10 'Do unto them what they want to do to you' is an old favourite of Jack's. It's clearly one of Sacchi's favourites as well. 'You're playing in front of them too much,' he would have said at half-time. 'You've got to start getting in behind and turning them round.' Evani, redundant in midfield is replaced by Massaro. They re-start, lift the pace significantly and set about turning us around. We concede a corner, then another. For fifteen minutes they dominate the show. Something is going to happen for them, you can sense it... and yet that final ball isn't working for them, those little one-twos at the edge of the box are not coming off. Paul is magnificent and Phil is rock solid in the middle for us; Terry and Denis are never run on the flanks. Packie makes a good save from Signori. Maybe it's not going to happen after all. Maybe we're not going to concede a goal.

17:32 We have our chances, too. Ray strikes a great right foot, better then he struck his goal, but Pagliuca is worthy this time and does well to save. The numbers go up on our touchline. Ray, who is still doing well against Maldini, is called in. His replacement is a cocky young man from Birkenhead who speaks with the typical scouser's tongue. There is a refreshing naivety about Jason McAteer. Here he is, thrown in at the deep end in his sixth cap for Ireland, and as he trots out to take on one of the best defenders in the world, his attitude is very much, 'Let's see how good you really are.' Within minutes, he is tormenting the Italians, slowly helping us turn around their earlier dominance.

17:45 The referee gives me a warning, 'Townsend, your goalkeeper,' referring to the time Packie is taking with his kicks. With ten minutes to go, it's true that time is slipping away now. I signal to Packie to speed things up. Then Tommy, who has worked ever so hard, goes down after an aerial clash with Baresi. Play is stopped and a stretcher brought on but, though slightly groggy after the accidental blow to the face, given a minute and a rub of Mick's sponge, Tommy will be fine. Only the referee won't wait a minute and, taking out his card, he books Tommy for refusing to be stretchered off the field.

17:54 Aldo runs on for Tommy, looking like he means business. One more minute then it's into injury time. The Italians finish with a flurry of corners but seem strangely reluctant to whip them in first time. They play it short, then out, then try to send it in again, but each time we manage to pump it clear. Forward again, this time with Donadoni slowly being closed by young Jason McAteer. Donadoni is under pressure, can't get his head up – he knows Baresi is with him, but with this bastard on his heels, he can't lift his head to see. Taking a chance that his captain is still free, he cuts the ball inside, but I've long seen it

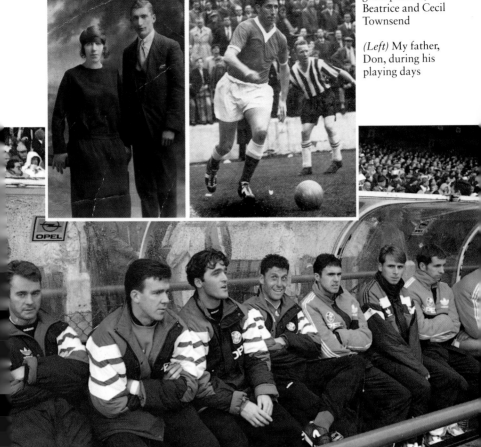

(Far left) My grandparents, Beatrice and Cecil Townsend

(Left) My father, Don, during his playing days

(Above) 'Always look on the bright side': sitting it out at Lansdowne Road after being substituted against Lithuania in September of '93. From left: John 'cheer up Shez' Sheridan, Alan Kelly, Eddie McGoldrick, myself, Alan McLoughlin, David Kelly and Chris Morris

(Left) Distracted by a voice in the crowd at Windsor Park in Belfast, November '93

(Below) 'America is this big.' Posing in Orlando before I decided to change my 'look'

(Below that) The amazing Mister Byrne: 'Andy I'm telling ye... you're the best... we're the best... we can't lose...'

Outside it's America. Channel cruising between the chat shows, game shows and baseball at the North Orlando Hilton

(Above) 'Jack you can't be serious, what do you mean we have no balls?' From left: Denis Irwin (obscured), Joe McGrath, myself, Tony Cascarino, Maurice Setters

(Top) Spot the Barney: Fred Flintstone gives the thumbs up to Steve Staunton's latest tie

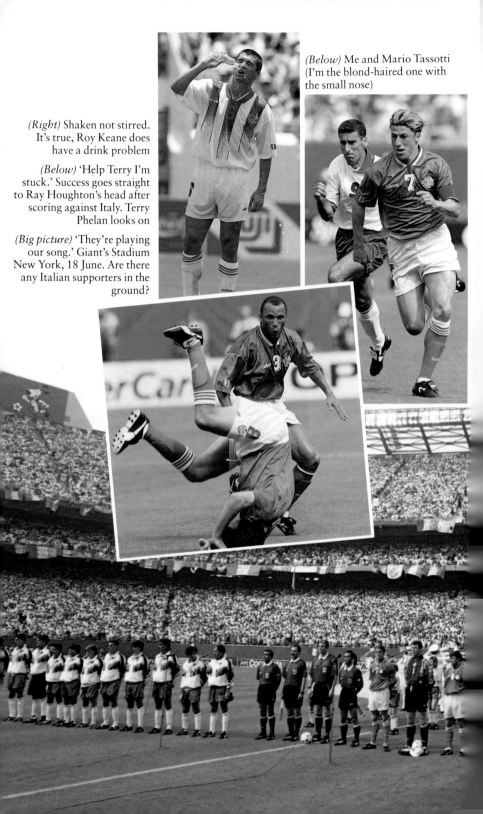

(Below) Me and Mario Tassotti (I'm the blond-haired one with the small nose)

(Right) Shaken not stirred. It's true, Roy Keane does have a drink problem

(Below) 'Help Terry I'm stuck.' Success goes straight to Ray Houghton's head after scoring against Italy. Terry Phelan looks on

(Big picture) 'They're playing our song.' Giant's Stadium New York, 18 June. Are there any Italian supporters in the ground?

(Left) Hat's off: Jack looks like he is about to throttle someone after the Mexican game

(Below) Norway's Goran Soerloth with the bit between his teeth

(Below left) 'Ground control to Major Tom.' Jack, Sean Connolly and John Charlton keep an eye on developments against Norway

Italy vs. Ireland   0:00

(Left) And now the end is here – a final wave to the fans after losing against Holland. 'See you in four years time… maybe'

'Man on'… oops, too late. Holland's Frank Rijkaard gets there first

(Below left) Tripartite committee? 'No, I don't want Albert's job.' Jack shares a joke with Taoiseach Albert Reynolds and Tanaiste Dick Spring

(Below) 'My girl' – Kelly catches 40 winks at the homecoming in the Phoenix Park

Stage fright: Pat Kenny finds me stuck for words at the Phoenix Park homecoming

Great to be home with Daniel, Jackie and Kelly

coming. Intercepting the pass, I sprint forward into their half and cannot believe it when I lift my head. Twenty players behind me, and just Gianluca Pagliuca standing between me and the Italian goal.

17:55 The weirdest thoughts flash through your brain at critical moments like this. One second I'm sprinting towards the Italian goal; the next I'm time-warped five years into the past to a summer's evening in May, a hotel called Finnstown House, and I'm a freshman on an Irish team striving to qualify for the World Cup. We are sitting watching the final act of the most extraordinary game of the season, the venue Anfield. The away team are Arsenal: after ninety minutes of play, the referee's whistle on the way to his mouth, they still need a goal to win the Championship. John Barnes has the ball, sprints down the wing and into the Arsenal half. The crowd, baying for a final whistle, suddenly switch and roar. Barnes has it. Surely he will end it now. He races to the by-line, whips in his cross – caught by David Seaman. The ref is glancing at his watch again, Seaman hoofs the ball down-field, Alan Smith flicks on... Mickey Thomas races on to it... *goooaaal*... Mickey Thomas scores. Back at a shocked Finnstown House, Jack is on his feet now, scathing of the error he believes has cost Liverpool the Championship. 'John Barnes,' he says, 'he's just bloody cost them the League.' We look at him, surprised, puzzled. He explains: 'He has the ball and loads of space and what does he do? Instead of running it into the corner and holding it up, he's gone for the kill and done something really silly. They've got it, booted it down-field and scored.'

17:55 Racing towards the Italian goal, I sense the posse closing behind. My legs have almost gone, but I'm close enough now. Pagliuca is in my sight. The target beckons – put this away and I'll never have to buy a drink in Ireland again – but so does Jack and the memory of John Barnes. 'He's just bloody cost them the League.' I change direction, opting for safety and the corner flag. Costacurta is first to arrive. I hold him off, then cruelly target his legs to win the touch. And the ball. We have the ball and that's all that matters. Because once we have the ball we have the game. Thank you, John Barnes.

18:01 We have the game. The lads run off the bench: hugs, high fives, slaps down the back, scenes of absolute delight. I look for Jackie in the crowd, give her a wave and begin the walk toward the tunnel. To my right I notice Jack, gesturing with three policeman who have flattened an Irish supporter attempting to run across the pitch (great tackle, in fairness, perhaps the best of the match). When I arrive, they've cuffed his hands, cut his lip and pinned him so hard to the turf that his nose has left a divot. Appealing for restraint, I advise the supporter to take it easy to avoid a rough ride but, face down with weight of three police-men on his spine, I think he had already drawn the same conclusion.

18:05 Just as I am about to step through our dressing-room door it dawns on me – I'm still wearing my shirt. Turning around, I head back towards the Italian quarters, where a somewhat dejected Signori is still clad in white. I ask: 'Swap shirts?' He's gracious in defeat, as indeed all the Italians were; we shake hands and, giving him a slap down the arm, I return to our dressing-room where congratulations are still flying around. Mick is crying his eyes out. Packie is emotional as well. The FAI are all shaking each other's hands and then the Taoiseach, Albert Reynolds, comes in. He walks over, shakes my hand and congratulates me on the game, and though I thank him, I'm not totally convinced he knows who I am. When we met in London recently, we'd got on to first name terms, but now... I don't know. Maybe it is the dye in my hair. I feel like saying, 'Er, Albert, it is me under here, you know.'

18:15 Tommy and Kev are picked to provide samples for dope control. Baresi, who has also been selected, is sitting alone and looking very dejected when they arrive. Telling me about it later, Kev said: 'When we went in and looked at him, he had "What the fuck am I doing here?" written all over his face. Because he had retired, hadn't he? He had seen it all and done it all and had retired – then someone talked him out of it and tempted him back. And now here he was... he looked like the loneliest figure in the world – amazing.' As it turned out, poor old Tom wasn't that far behind in the dejection stakes. Sick from heat exhaustion and dry as a fig, he took two hours to provide a sample and was one of the last to leave the ground.

19:00 We are now united with our wives and a party has been laid on, a short drive away from the ground. Tired and still sweating from our efforts, what we need right now is an air conditioned room, somewhere we can sit and relax in comfort with family and friends. But what we get is quite amazing, even for the FAI. Pulling up at a dog track, half a mile from the ground, we step off the coach and are frog-marched to a tent through thousands of partying fans, who have gathered for a concert. Though not exactly the type of air conditioning we had in mind, at first the tent is fine. Sipping a beer, I stand with Jackie, my brother Mike and Larry Mullen from U2, talking about the day and the excitement of the game. After ten minutes, however, you cannot move: supporters, piling in the door, have decided the main event is 'inside'. After half an hour of 'Can you sign this Andy' and 'Great game Andy', I'm feeling absolutely shitty and decide to return to the sanctuary of the bus.

19:31   As I make my way back through the crowd, a supporter stops me and congratulates me on the game. A Chelsea fan, he asks what so many other supporters of the club have asked since I left for Aston Villa: how could I? Tempted to linger and explain, I shrug it off and move on. Yet it bothers me. I've been painted as the villain of the piece, but so much of what went on was never explained.

20:00   There are no celebrations on the way to the airport. Delighted as we are with the result, everyone is just too knackered to sing or dance. Personally, I'm beginning to feel 'iffy' now. Weak and sweating, I am bordering on the sick. The bus arrives at Newark airport – not at the terminal building itself but at some customs gate around the back. Very Important People, we are to be driven directly to the foot of the stairway leading to plane – the normal formalities don't apply. Except that the plane, our plane, the one that has been especially chartered to whizz our team back to Orlando, hasn't arrived, has it? It's up there in the sky taking some other suckers for a ride. So, two hours after the greatest game of our lives, here we are, sitting on a bus outside the gate of Newark airport. The service gate. Very important people, you understand....

22:00   Whose fault is this? Why wasn't this bloody plane waiting when we arrived? If we were the Italian team it would have been. If I was Baresi, I'd have stepped off the coach, on to the plane and before I had buckled my seat-belt – zoooom, we'd have been gone. We wouldn't have been taken to no dog track. We wouldn't still be sitting on the ramp waiting for people I have never seen in my life to board our VIP plane.

23:00   I sip from a beer but don't really want it. Dinner arrives on a tray and tastes like shit. Thirty-three thousand feet high is not where I want to be at this time. I am tired, sick, feel a migraine coming on. I long for a room, an air conditioned room. Some space. A bed, my bed. I long to be anywhere else in the world but here.

01:45 The nightmare continues when we arrive at the Hilton in Orlando. I can't quite believe my eyes – all these people clapping, strange people, ears, costumes, make-up, masks, silver hair, silver faces, thigh-length silver boots…. 'It's a *Star Trek* convention,' someone says. I can see the headlines tomorrow: 'Spock, Scotty and James T. Kirk welcome the Irish team back to their hotel.' Anxious to be free of these freaks, I make for the room with Jackie, but we are accosted by six Kling-ons in the lift. 'Beam me up,' one says as I punch the eighth floor. Have you ever heard such crap? Cass and his wife Sarah invite us to join them at the bar for a drink, but I'm gone. My head is lifting. All I want now is to close the door and shut out the world until tomorrow… which is actually today.

Some like it hot

Mexico
(June 19 to June 25)

DAY 14

SUNDAY JUNE 19:

DIRE STRAITS

Morning. I opened my eyes. The little gap in the curtains said 'blue skies'. That's nice. I dozed for a while, let the data settle – where I am, what I'm doing here, why I feel good about the day before – then threw back the sheets and placed my feet on the floor. My legs were stiff, my joints sore. Nothing that isn't normal on the morning after a game, except for this rash – this rash on my knee, an itchy redness that had puffed up my right knee-cap and the back of my leg as well. It was a mosquito bite; I was sure of it. Using the repellant that had been left beside each bed, I sprayed both my legs and, feigning panic, called Jackie from the shower: 'Jackie! Take a look at this, quick. I think I'm being attacked by the flesh-eating bug.'

We slipped down to breakfast, not many of the lads around. Jack had stayed up north for the Norway-Mexico game (in Washington) and we'd been given the day off. Returning to the room, I applied some Sudocream to what was now, I decided, a heat rash, then ordered a taxi. Jackie's mum, her brother, and her mum's friend, who arrived yesterday with our children Daniel and Kelly, have rented an apartment in a place called Kissimee and we were going to spend the day with them. Jackie, Sarah Cascarino and Stan's fiancée Joanne, who will all be banned from the team hotel once the curfew drops this evening, have rented alongside.

Turning left off Route 486, we found heavy traffic heading west on Interstate 4 and ground to a halt on the outskirts of Orlando. Our driver, who spoke with a strong southern drawl, was miffed: 'Hellll, I don't know what's wrong with this traffic today. Shouldn't be too looong.' He sat back, tapped his wheel, incredibly laid back. I mean, if this was a London cabby, he would have come off and double-backed and known at least three alternative ways of getting to Kissimee. But then, if this was London he would have known not to take the highway in the first place. He would have known about the game (Belgium v Morocco) in town today, would have known about the World Cup.

Cars with steaming radiators littered the hard shoulder. It was an extremely hot day, and the air conditioning in the taxi struggled to keep us cool. We crawled forward, eventually broke free. He radioed for directions to the address we'd given him – Dyer Square. 'They can't find this place,' he explained. My nerves were starting to fray. It was three weeks since I'd seen my kids and it was Daniel's eighth birthday, but at the rate we were progressing I wasn't going to make the cake. 'Pull over if you see a phone,' I suggested to the driver. 'I've a number I can ring.' Ramming eight quarters into the slot when I only needed one, I dialled the head office of the agency that had rented us the apartments. 'Can you give this driver directions to Dyer Square please?' I asked, handing him the phone. It turned out that the address we had been given had been abbreviated – we needed to go to Dyer Square, Dyer Boulevard. 'Hellll, I know Dyer Boulevard,' our driver said, offloading his guilt. I bit my tongue – it *is* Sunday – and ten minutes later we arrived.

The afternoon was ultimately disappointing. Having planned to do so much, we ended up doing little. Four-year-old Kelly, delighted to have her Daddy back, wanted to show him how good she can swim. Goggles on, splashing around, across and under the water. Each time he decided he had had enough of the pool, she took hold of his hand and showed him 'what else' she could do. He played for an hour. And then another. But it was a chore. Absolutely drained from his efforts of the day before, try as he did, he just wasn't much fun....

Shortly after two, we took the kids to the other apartment. Stan was there with Joanne, but with nothing in the place to eat, the girls immediately set off for the shops, leaving Stan and me with the golf (the final round of the US Open). I wasn't sure how long I had slept when I woke up. Stan had gone, crashed out in one of the bedrooms, and I dozed for a while longer until Jackie and Jo came home. Dan asked if I could take him to Universal Studios, but settled instead for a game of ball with the Houghton boys – James, Brett and Anthony, who are staying just around the corner. Kelly was whacked. I took her into her bedroom, give her a cuddle and within two minutes she was gone.

Feeling better for my own nap, I appreciated the cool of the evening. I considered staying, would have liked to spend the night with my family, but midnight was the curfew and it didn't seem right to abuse Jack's trust. Ray called over around ten. We called a cab and then decided to stop off in Church Street (Orlando's main thoroughfare) for a quick beer. Mulvaney's was packed. Aldo, Ronnie and Roy had obviously been there a while, for all three seemed... well... buoyant, so to speak. We sat down and ordered a beer, but I wasn't comfortable, was becoming more and more concerned about the heat and swelling in my knee.

'Naaah, don't worry, it will be all right,' Ray said.

'Yeah, it's nothing,' Stan agreed.

I wasn't convinced. 'Listen, it's twice the size of the other one and getting bigger as we talk. I want to get back.'

Finishing my drink, I borrowed the fare from Stan for the taxi to the Hilton. Martin Walsh, the team doctor, wasn't there when I arrived, but Larry (Larry Quinn, one of our helpers) said he would wait for him in the lobby and bring him up when he got in. Larry brought me some ice and, packing it around the swelling, I sat down to watch TV. Then Martin knocked on the door: 'Oh Christ, you've got some sort of allergy. You'll need tablets and some cream, but within two or three days you should be okay.'

⚽   ⚽   ⚽

'Blue is the colour...'

By the summer of 1990, after two happy but unsuccessful years at Norwich, my career had taken off and I was ready for bigger things. While Everton's Colin Harvey and Arsenal's George Graham both made inquiries, Chelsea's Bobby Campbell was the most dogged. Phoning me at home one afternoon, he asked, 'What are you doing with yourself in the summer, son?'

'Well,' I said,' I'm going to Italy for the World Cup and am basically going to keep my options open until I get back.'

'Okay, that's good to hear. But you're coming to Chelsea, make no mistake about it. I told my chairman you're the man I want and he's coming to get you. I should have got you two years ago. You're coming to play for me, son.'

Thanking him for his interest, I turned the negotiation over to John Mac, my agent, who had talks with the clubs concerned and reported back with the results.

'Look,' he said, 'Chelsea really want you and are prepared to pay, and you'll be much better off if you go and play for them.'

'What about Robert Chase [the Norwich chairman]?' I asked. 'Has everything been cleared with him?'

'Yes. They've virtually agreed a fee. So if you want, we can go and speak to them.'

'Okay, let's do it,' I replied.

A week after the season ended in May, I got into my car and drove from Norwich to the St Albans junction of the M25. John Mac, Bobby Campbell and his assistant Gwyn Williams were at the Swallow Hotel when I arrived. We sat down, had a brief discussion, and while John and Bobby peeled off to sort out the nitty gritty, Gwyn and I had a chat about old times. From the time I was a boy, you see, Chelsea were always 'my' club; Stamford Bridge was a forty-minute drive from our home in Bexleyheath and Dad would occasionally take me in to see a game.

'Blue is the colour, football is the....'

Although I had trained for them a couple of times as a schoolboy, the closest I ever came to signing was at the age of seventeen. Invited, in the summer of 1980, to attend their pre-season training camp at Aberystwyth in Wales, I spent a week running up and down sand dunes with the 'stars' – Micky Droy, Clive Walker and Kevin Hales – and even played alongside them for half a game. I'll never forget how good I felt that day pulling on the Chelsea strip. Although it was their away kit (white), it was as if I had just been handed a million dollars. I played okay in the game; didn't try to do anything special other than keep my nose clean. Gwyn Williams, who was the youth-team coach at the time, announced the 'verdict' as soon as we returned to London.

'You've got a job, haven't you?' he began.

'Yeah, at Greenwich Council, that's right.'

'Right. Well with your part-time football and your job and every-thing else, we're probably not going to be able to pay you what you're earning now, if we decide to sign you up.' As soon as he said 'if', I immediately understood that they didn't really think I was good enough. I could have signed – they would certainly have given me the chance – but some of Mum's old caution had rubbed off and I wasn't prepared to forfeit what I had for buttons.

The wheeling and dealing over this time around, John spelt out the figures: 'XYZ, four-year contract, you're going to earn good money.'

'What about Arsenal?' I said. 'What are we doing with Arsenal?'

'How do you mean?'

'Well, surely if there's another team interested, it is in our interest to get an auction going here?'

This probably sounds quite mercenary, but I must explain that a larger pay packet wasn't my only goal here. After five years as a professional, the centre of the doughnut was all I had ever won as far as honours were concerned, and the idea of playing for Arsenal – the League champions of the previous season – did appeal to me.

However, John was adamant: 'Andy, they want to do it today. They want to take you from here to Stamford Bridge to do the medical and then back to the office to sign.'

I wasn't happy, wanted time to think it over. I mean, with another year of my Norwich contract still to run, there was no pressure on me to sign. Okay, the offer on the table was good, but I didn't desperately need to accept it. The argument continued.

'Look, I think out of courtesy you should at least ring the other mob.'

'Andy, Bobby Campbell's been in the game for years and years, and if I go out there and tell him I want to make a few calls, he'll know what we're at. Now, do you want to play for Chelsea or don't you?'

Did I? Boxed further into a corner, I'm sure that if it hadn't been for my affection for the club I would probably have stood up and walked out. But the more I imagined myself in the Chelsea colours, the more it felt like the right thing to do. I rang Jackie, explained the position and when she said, 'It's up to you,' my mind was clear.

'Okay,' I told Bobby Campbell. 'Let's do it, fine.'

The medical was a formality. A new set of contact lenses ensured I didn't have to cheat the eye-test, and the only surprise was when the doctor requested a sample of blood for an Aids test. The examination complete, it was time to sign the contract.

In accordance with the wishes of Robert Chase (who was wary, perhaps, of the effect on pre-season ticket sales if he was seen to be selling off some of his better players), it was agreed to keep the deal secret until after the World Cup. Led to an old house that was covered in ivy climbers, I was welcomed first by Colin Hutchinson, the managing director, and then by the chairman, Ken Bates.

'Welcome to Chelsea,' the chairman greeted. 'You'll enjoy it here. It's a great club and I hope you have a long and successful stay.'

'Thanks very much,' I replied. 'Pleasure to be here.' It was.

Stamford Bridge is not the most attractive football ground in England. It's not Old Trafford or White Hart Lane or Highbury, but there is a magic about it that only those who have ever loved the club can appreciate. As a result, perhaps, of my own feeling for the place, my first season at Chelsea (1990–91), was the best of my life. Installed as captain just two months after my debut, I responded with a string of performances that were as good as any other midfielder in the country and fired as much by passion as heart and legs.

There was just one problem. I was turning it on in what was, basically, an average team. Also-rans in the League (eleventh), we were eliminated by Oxford (3–1) in our first match of the FA Cup and reached the semi-finals of the League Cup, only to be slaughtered by Sheffield Wednesday over two legs. The Wednesday defeat was undoubtedly the low point of the year; sitting in the dressing-room at Hillsborough as chants of 'Heigh-ho-super-Wednesday' rang round the ground, I felt gutted. For the fifth time in my career, I had fallen at the final hurdle before a Wembley final.

Solutions weren't easy. At a time when we needed to be strengthening the side, most attention seemed focused on the need to secure the ground. Every day the papers were full of it: 'Such and such a consortium are about to buy it', 'Chelsea are moving to Craven Cottage', 'Stamford Bridge has been sold', 'Stamford Bridge has been saved'. So much so that, exasperated, I can remember arguing with Bobby Campbell about it.

'Look,' I said, 'sod the ground; we need players, we want to win something here. The fans don't need elevators to take them to seats in a fancy new stand – they'll stand behind a piece of rope if necessary. They want a team, something to bloody cheer about.'

Looking back, however, I know it wasn't as simple as that. Money was obviously tight, for although the squad was boosted by a couple of good signings, it was weakened by the transfer of others who should never have been allowed to go.

If the season was personally a rewarding and satisfying one for me, then it ended on a very odd note. At the end of a function where the chairman presented me with the Player of the Year award, I was given a message by one of the stewards that 'the gaffer wanted to see me out in the car park in his car'. When I went outside, Bobby Campbell's BMW was parked not far from the door, his wife driving. Bobby, sitting beside her in the front passenger seat, wound down his window when I approached.

'All right, boss? What's the problem?' I asked.

His wife was crying. 'You know what they've done to him, don't you?' she sobbed.

'No,' I replied, 'I don't...' until suddenly it dawned on me that the chairman had given him the shove.

'What's the matter? What's happening?' I asked.

'Don't worry about it,' Bobby replied. 'I'm sorry, Andy. Look, I'll be in touch, I'll speak to you soon.' Then he turned to his wife and asked her to take them home.

The next day, word filtered down that Bobby Campbell hadn't been sacked at all, but simply moved aside. Reaction in the dressing-room was mixed. While there were one or two like myself who were sorry to see him 'go', there were others who were clearly delighted. It's that sort of job, that sort of game.

I was driving around in London on the day it was announced that Ian Porterfield would be the new Chelsea manager. I drove straight to the ground, shook his hand and wished him luck in his new job. Ian, of course, was no stranger to Chelsea and had been Bobby's assistant for a spell before taking the manager's job at Reading. It was a very popular choice in the dressing-room, where he was known affectionately as 'Porters', and we kicked off 1991–92 with a spirit in the team that I hadn't known before – so much so that I actually used to look forward each morning to driving in to work.

On the transfer front, the side was both strengthened (Vinnie Jones) and weakened (Tony Dorigo, Gordon Durie), but the season started so well for me (five goals in the first six weeks) and I was enjoying it so much that the comings and goings didn't bother me. What did bother me, however, was that I had fallen down the pecking order as far as wages were concerned. When I mentioned this to Ian, he arranged for me to meet the chairman to sort out a new deal.

Before we sat down to lunch in his favourite Italian restaurant, I'd never had much to do with Ken Bates. I'd heard a good deal about him, though, and knew he wasn't the type for pussyfooting around. Lunch reinforced these impressions. Once a small Italian waiter had ushered us to his favourite table, we sat down, were handed menus, and while I sat there trying to make sense of something like *Brushetta taglierini al profumo di limone*, the chairman ordered – for both of us.

'Right then, you're looking for a new deal,' he said, looking me straight in the eye.

'Yeah, I am. Look, I love it here and I....'

'What do you want? Five years? What sort of money are you looking for?'

'Well, Gordon Durie's just gone to Spurs and I know he's on a lot more than me, and Tony Dorigo's has gone to Leeds and I know he's doing better there as well, so....'

'What sort of figures?'

I told him.

'Okay,' he said, 'fine. We'll get that drawn up and signed when we get back.'

And that was it. The deal had been done and dusted before we had even tackled our starters. We returned to the club after lunch, and once the new contract had been drawn and signed, some details were released to the press. 'Townsend commits himself to Chelsea for the remainder of his career,' was the gist of most of the stories – stories I've been reminded of many times since coming to Aston Villa. Chelsea fans, you see, never forget. Nor should they, but there's so much they don't understand. There is so much I don't understand. From being almost blissfully happy to be wearing the Chelsea colours, overnight the tide just seemed to turn.

 **DAY 15**

MONDAY JUNE 20:
GRAZIE SACCHI

My legs are a mess. The right, from knee to ankle, is double its normal size; the back of the left is red raw and oozing pus. Various theories abound as to the source. One of the security guys attached to the team believes it to be 'poison ivy'. Martin, the doctor, is sticking to his allergy theme. The lads (surprise, surprise) have suggested everything from Aids to gonorrhoea. Mick thinks it's the spray, the mosquito repellant: 'Alan McLoughlin used it on his forehead and shoulder last week and came out in a horrible rash.' We were in his treatment room now and, having smeared the cortisone cream like butter over the mess, he was preparing to compress it with some iced towels. Picking up the spray while he applied the first of the towels, I scanned the label for clues, but was at a loss. 'What bloody ridiculous stuff! You spray it on your legs and it does this to you! Made in Italy, then, was it? Sent to us compliments of the Italian team?'

The lads split into two groups this morning. Those who didn't play on Saturday went to the training ground with Jack, the rest to a nearby health club for just a swim and jacuzzi. As I sat with my legs up for the rest of the day, a phone call from Jackie and the US Open play-off between Ernie Els, Lauren Roberts and Colin Montgomery were my only diversions. Not exactly the most memorable day so far.

⚽　　⚽　　⚽

...Business is the game
Groin strains are a bit like toothaches – you can postpone the visit to the dentist only for so long. A few weeks after my Italian lunch with Chelsea chairman Ken Bates, I realised with great pain that it was time for me to face the inevitable. I'd known about my double hernia from early in the season, but had hoped to postpone the operation until the season's end in June. However, on the night of October 23, when I quite literally seized up while warming up for a Zenith Cup game

against Swindon Town, I realised I would have to succumb sooner rather than later and immediately fixed a date. My brief sojourn at the Princess Grace hospital was a peaceful, if painful time. On the night before my operation, the nurse – a South African who insisted on calling me Andrew – tucked me in with some final instructions.

'Now then, Andrew, here is your razor for the shave. We'll be coming to get you at seven tomorrow morning.' Complying, I was up at half past six next morning, but wondered why on earth it was so important for me to shave. I mean, it wasn't as if I had a particularly heavy growth or anything. Did I really look that bad?

The nurse arrived at the appointed hour. 'Have you had your shave?' she asked.

'Just finishing,' I replied, wiping the mousse from my face.

'No, down below,' she said, emphasising the 'below'. 'Have you had a shave down below?'

'Sorry…. No. I'll do it straight away,' I answered, feeling like a right prat.

I retreated into the cubicle, and once I had performed the necessary, I removed my contact lenses before turning on the shower. Now, without my contact lenses I'm the original Mister Magoo, and while reaching for what I expected to be a bar of soap, I stubbed my thumb on the Wilkinson Sword and all but hacked it off. Stemming the cascade of blood with a huge wad of toilet paper, I must have looked a right sight as I stepped from the shower.

'Oh dear,' the nurse said. 'What have you done?'

Wheeled into the operating theatre, I was knocked out (as much, I suspect, to protect me from myself as anything else), cut open, repaired and sewn up. When I awoke, the eminent Dr Gilmore, whose pioneering surgery in the domain has saved many a player's career, was there at the end of the bed. 'Everything went fine,' he said. 'You're all done. I've even put two stitches in your thumb.'

The operation, in hindsight, was perhaps the turning point. I was eager to return to the side as quickly as possible, but four weeks was a little too quick (the average recovery time is six to eight weeks), and I struggled to find the same edge as before. Christmas approached. Results were average. Still searching for a vein of good form, I felt more responsible than any other player for the performances of the team. In previous years, I had never been too demanding on myself – if I played well, I played well.

If I didn't, I didn't. However, as captain of Chelsea, 'my' club, there were demands, responsibilities, an obligation almost, to perform.

It was around this time – Christmas of '91 – when rumours began to circulate that the chairman wanted to get rid of me. Absolutely flabbergasted, at first I didn't believe them. Not much more than two months previously, Ken Bates had given me a five-year deal. Why on earth should he suddenly change his mind?

A possible clue to the sudden change in policy 'upstairs' came through a conversation I had a few days later with managing director Colin Hutchinson. I was pulling his leg over something or other when he said, jokingly: 'Yeah, you got your new deal all signed up and then had your operation done.' And though I laughed at the time, the remark immediately stuck. Did they seriously believe the two were related? Had the operation and subsequent drop in my form provoked some sudden re-evaluation of my worth? A five-year contract was a considerable investment. Did it suddenly make more sense to sell rather than keep me on? Unable to make any sense of it, I decided to go directly to the man who could.

Accompanied by Ian Porterfield, I met Ken Bates in the board-room after a game.

'Are you looking to sell me, or not?' I asked. 'I'd like to know straight.'

'No, I'm not,' he replied.

'Well, how come I keep hearing from people that you are?'

'Well, who have you been hearing it from?'

'A million and one different people.'

'No,' he repeated. 'I am not looking to sell you.'

The conversation shifted, but my mind was still buzzing. Not at all convinced, I felt like I had just been sentenced to death row. The remainder of the season was miserable. Alex Ferguson made contact and, for a while, a move to Manchester United looked a possibility. I considered submitting a transfer request, but didn't see why I should have to pay when they were the ones who wanted me out the door.

Ian was adamant I should stay. He was very good like that. I'm only sorry I never played better for him and that the team never played better for him. I feel quite bitter about it, looking back; I mean, there were players on long-term contracts who wouldn't have given two shits if the place had gone down the tubes. And there I was, a true believer, and they wanted to let me go. Blowing hot and cold for the rest of the season, I wasn't the same.

My third and final season at Chelsea (1992–93) was more of the same. We had been going quite well in the League coming up to Christmas, but then, in the space of a few days in January, the arse totally fell out of the year. In the third round (our first) of the FA Cup, away to Middlesbrough, we were leading 1–0 with ten minutes to go when Middlesbrough scored twice to send us out. A few days later, we played Crystal Palace on a rain-sodden night in the quarter-finals of the League Cup. We played great, I scored a great goal... but we were beaten 3–1 in a game we could easily have won 6–3.

That defeat weighed heavy on the team and spelt the end for Ian when it was followed by a dismal run in the League. David Webb was brought in to keep the ship afloat, and did so until the end of the season, when the job was offered to Glenn Hoddle. Hugely respected as he is within the game, Hoddle's was a great appointment and in different circumstances I'm sure I could have played well for him. But too much water had passed under the bridge for me to stay.

Another factor was a personal need for change. In eight seasons with three First Division clubs, I had played in five Cup semi-finals but won nothing. I felt I was beginning to stagnate and that a bigger club would provide a fresh challenge, the required kick in the pants, and at thirty years of age it was now or never. Summer holidays that year were spent, oddly enough, in this place – Orlando – but as soon as I returned I asked to see my new manager.

'No-one,' I explained, 'has played more games in my three years here. Irrespective of whatever you hear from anybody else, Glenn, I've given my best for Chelsea and I'm gutted at the fact that I'm sitting here now, telling you I want to leave, but I do. Too much has happened. I've had Bobby Campbell, Gwyn Williams, Ian Porterfield, Stan Ternant [Ian's first assistant], Don Howe [Ian's second assistant], Dave Webb and now you... in three seasons! My brain's gone a bit. I've seen enough and heard too much, and I don't think you'll get the best out of me as a player, so I want to go.'

'Andy, I appreciate what you're saying,' he replied, 'and I understand it. But for me to get rid of the captain, five minutes after coming in the door – that puts me in an awkward position.'

Of the four clubs that were showing an interest in me – Aston Villa, Everton, Manchester City and Sheffield Wednesday – Villa attracted me most. Runners-up in the Championship the season before, they played an exciting brand of football and I liked the idea of linking up with Ray, Stan and Paul. Concerned that the asking price (£2 million) was too much, I was delighted when Glenn gave me the green light to go and speak with Big Ron.

'But I'd like you do me a favour,' he said. 'I'm not asking you to put in a transfer request, but I'd like you to say you wanted to leave, because you're the one they idolise around here and that will make it a whole lot easier for me.'

'Okay,' I said. 'Yeah, I'll do that – for you.'

So after I spoke to Ron and the deal was signed, when the question was aired in my dealings with the press, I made sure to mention that I 'wanted' to leave – which, in a way, was true, but in another, false. I left to win trophies, but also because the feeling I had felt for the club had been ripped out.

For our first meeting in the League, Chelsea travelled up to Villa Park. While I never expected to have roses thrown at me, to be booed so vociferously by supporters I had once had a great relationship with really hurt – much more than I could have imagined. Seven months later, however, when I walked up the steps at Wembley to collect my first winner's medal after our 3–1 victory over Manchester United in the League Cup final, I knew I had made the right decision. Seven weeks later, Chelsea, ironically enough, also made it to Wembley. Conscious of how much that would have meant to all the old faithfuls at the club, I was genuinely sorry to see them lose.

A couple of months after joining Villa, I was sitting having a cup of tea with Jackie after training one day when I said, quite out of the blue: 'You know, if I was ever asked to be captain, I don't think I would really want to know. I just want to try and do well here and play out my days and be happy.' And I meant it. It's true, because while captaining Ireland is a great honour, at club level it can be a terrible strain. At Chelsea I got to hear too much about players and people – things you didn't always want to hear. I loved the club, loved the supporters, but it's nice to be able to play without that burden now.

That three-year spell at Chelsea summed up a lot of what I despise about the game. Loyalty to the club is all very fine, but at the end of the day, when your 'star' begins to fade, it doesn't count for much. A player's ultimate loyalty must be to his family, himself. For all those who run the modern game, all he really is, is figures on a ledger – a business transaction.

DAY 16

TUESDAY JUNE 21:

300 WEST ROBINSON STREET

Doctor José Lara, a FIFA-approved dermatologist at the local hospital, blew the Italian conspiracy theory. 'What you have,' he said, lifting his studied brow from the layer of seeping crocodile hide that was once a hairy shin, 'is contact dermatitis, which basically is an allergy to something you have come in contact with.' Prescribing a stronger cortisone cream to be applied thrice daily with the cold-compress towels, he suggested that a shot in the bum of the same (cortisone) might speed the process up. However, our team doctors, Martin and Conal Hooper, argued against this. With our second game against Mexico just three days away, it would be silly to run the risk of being caught at dope control. We returned to the hotel, where Mick broke out the butter knife for a fresh spread. The lads, given the day off, were cruising Daytona Beach. But did I feel hard done by?

Clutching the address I had ripped from the Yellow Pages, I jumped into the taxi.

'Where do you wanna go, sir?' the lady driver asked.

'To 300 West Robinson Street.'

'Three hundred West Robinson Street?'

'That's right, yeah.'

'Naah, you must have the wrong address, what ye got there?'

I showed her the address. T-h-r-e-e h-u-n-d-r-e-d W-e-s-t R-o-b-i-n-s-o-n.

'You do realise that's a black neighbourhood, don't you, sir?'

'Well no, I didn't actually. Eh, is that likely to cause any problems?'

She paused, thought about it. 'Naah, you should be all right.'

Driving off, we took the same route to Orlando – left off 486 for Interstate 4 or 'eye-four' as it is known locally – but were thirty minutes quicker, it being mid-afternoon. When we arrived, West Robinson Street was pretty much as she had painted it. For black neighbourhood read low-quality housing, tired old gas-guzzling 'Cads' and shop-fronts you don't find on the fashionable side of town. Stepping from the car in my T-shirt, shorts and flip-flops, the only white person around, I actually felt quite alien. And vulnerable, very vulnerable. With filofax and credit cards in my hand, if it came to making a run for it I'd be in real trouble.

'Could you wait for me?' I asked, handing her the fare.

'I'm sorry... not in this neighbourhood.'

(Oh great). 'Okay, well then, could you come back and pick me up in, say, half an hour?'

'Sure.'

She drove off. I turned around. Pulling back the door, I stepped inside.

⚽　　⚽　　⚽

Five years ago, when Jackie was pregnant with Kelly, we took the car to Great Yarmouth for the day. One of the things we liked most about our two years at Norwich was its proximity to the sea: when morning cloud gave way to sun in the afternoon, you could have your sleeves up at the beach just thirty minutes later. Returning to the car one day after a pleasant stroll in the sand, we were browsing in shop windows when we saw this beautiful guitar.

'I'd love to be able to play one of them,' I said to Jackie.

'Really? Why don't you learn?'

'Well, I don't know. I've never felt really musically inclined. I just don't feel I've any real talent for it, but I'd love to learn – shall I get one and have a go?'

'Yeah, why not?'

The strings were so hard they blistered my fingers at first, but I practised and practised, determined to get some return for my hundred pounds investment. The how-to-play book came free. I was getting nowhere fast, so some lessons were suggested and a Ben Elton look-alike called Alan agreed to teach me. On my first night, he threw my book in the bin and said the guitar would have to go. 'You'll have more fun with an electric one,' he said. 'Acoustics are for people who can play.' I liked him. Two days later, I'd traded in my old/new one and was strumming a Fender Stratocaster or 'Strat' as we say in the trade. Learning the various chords came first. Then it was time to massacre a tune. 'We'll start you on "Suspicious Minds" by Elvis and Monty Python's "Always Look on the Bright Side" – they're good learning songs, lots of changing chords,' he said. Always look on the bright side? Did he have any idea how I made my living? Was he taking the piss?

One lesson led to another and slowly I began to progress. Like the kid who can't wait to tell his mum about what he has just discovered in school, I would race home after lessons, break out the guitar and say, 'Jackie, do you remember I used to do this?' (strumming a few chords). 'Well, what I should really have being doing is this.' And she would look at me, with eyes that said 'Have you lost your head?' and say, 'Oh, that's really good that is.' But soon the practice paid off and I did begin to play better. Lost to another world whenever I decided to play, I found that if what came out wasn't always musical, it was, and still is, the perfect therapy for me.

⚽   ⚽   ⚽

From the moment I pushed through the door, Guitars Plus was everything you would expect a music shop in a 'black neighbourhood' to be. An old boy, sitting with his legs crossed just inside the door, looked me up and down. Guitar as old as himself in his lap, fingers like sausages – as they walked lazily up and down the fret board, the sound of his blues was slow and relaxing. Giving him a nod as I stepped past, I was just about to begin my tour when this big guy from behind the counter with the complete accent asked: 'Wha kinna gee-taa ye lookin fo' man?'

If there is one thing that gets my back up when I walk into shops it's being hounded. Car salesmen are models for it. I remember walking into this Jaguar-Daimler showroom one afternoon when I was at Chelsea. I hadn't shaved and was dressed casually in a track suit and runners and, of course, I hadn't put my foot on the carpet but this suit had come racing across. 'Can I help you with anything, sir?'

Now, for once, I hadn't come to look around; the car of my dreams was sitting under this roof and I had the cheque in my pocket to pay for it. But he didn't know that, did he? Having judged me on my appearance, he wanted to get my arse out the door as fast as possible and point me to the second-hand yard. Aware of his discomfort, I decided to play him along. Running my fingers along the bonnet of a gleaming light-blue XJS, I asked, 'How much for one of these?'

Expecting me to move along, he said, 'That, sir, will cost you £29,000.'

'And what sort of deal will you give me for cash?'

He was surprised, not yet convinced. 'Well, it depends on....'

'I'll pay you today. I'll pay you now.'

Total disbelief: 'What?'

'But I want it taxed and ready to drive first thing in the morning.'

Well, that look in his face when he realised I was serious – it was worth every penny.

Meanwhile, back in Guitars Plus....

'Wha kinna gee-taa ye lookin fo' man?'

I told him I wasn't actually looking for anything in particular, just having a browse around, and he nodded in acknowledgement. There was none of the candy-sweet 'Well if you need any help, sir, you know how to find me' talk you get in other American stores. I was free to browse at last, two ten-year-old boys the only other customers. The place was big and open, and there wasn't a lot of equipment. If this had been a shop back home, there would be three or four TVs showing promotional videos and five or six different sound-proof booths where you could retire in peace and 'test-strum' what you fancied. Here, the old man playing blues was the shop's only promotion and most of the equipment was second-hand. Still, it certainly had character and the sheet music was good. I bought a couple of books, came out after twenty-five minutes and the taxi was there.

'Sorry to keep you waiting. Everything okay?'

'Yeah, fine. I've just been here a couple of minutes. Don't like hanging around. Where to?'

'The Hilton.'

 **DAY 17**

WEDNESDAY JUNE 22:

'COME IN JOHN STARKS
YOUR TIME IS UP'

José Lara's extra-strong cream seems to be doing its stuff. Although my shin is still very swollen, the fluid has gone from around the knee and the rash is not nearly as raw today.

After three days of sitting around, I was keen to join the lads for the midday session at the Citrus Bowl. Martin Walsh advised that I keep my legs covered, and though I didn't feel that comfortable, the session went okay. Although Jack's philosophy, now that the tournament has started, is rest, rest, rest between games, it was nice to get out for a run-around. Although not nearly as impressive a venue as the Giants Stadium, the surface was possibly better – absolutely immaculate. We didn't do that much – a few shots at goal – forty minutes of what wasn't so much a game as a shuffle up and down the pitch and that's it.

This evening, there were one or two problems to be sorted out with the FAI. In the past, I've tended to leave that sort of thing to Ray and Kevin, but Kevin has been at me recently to play a more active role. He's right – as captain I should be more involved – so this evening I joined him and Ray for a discussion with Joe Delaney over something that had seriously peeved us about the Italian game.

On the night before the game, when we were given our (two) complimentary tickets, one or two of the lads remarked that the categories weren't the same. While some were Category 1 (the best seats in the house), others were 2 or 3, and they were all scattered at random around the ground. A little bit annoyed, when we walked out and lined up for the national anthems the following day, I noticed a couple of the Italian players waving to some people in the crowd. Now, to be truthful, I couldn't tell Mrs Donadoni from Mrs Baresi, but I do know they were sitting together halfway up the middle tier – with Mrs Pagliuca and Mrs Berti and all the other wives – in the best seats in the house. Now again, to be fair, my own wife Jackie and brother Mike weren't that far away from them. But that's not the point. Ronnie Whelan's mother and brother were down behind a corner flag somewhere and Alan McLoughlin's wife was up with the gods. That's not right. We deserve better.

This evening we tackled Joe Delaney about it. 'What's the arrangements for Friday?' we asked.

He took out this piece of paper, a map of the Citrus Bowl and handed it to us. 'They're all Category 1 tickets,' he assured us.

'What are all these crosses, Joe?' Kev asked, examining the paper.

'That's the position of the seats as they've been advanced.'

'But they're not all together!'

'Well, this is how they've arrived. They arrived from FIFA like this – we only got them today.'

Venting our dissatisfaction, we examined the map and the box of tickets on the table containing what was left of the FAI's allocation and, after half an hour of juggling, at last arrived at a situation where our families would be seated together. But it does make me wonder why we were here arguing about it. Surely something so basic should be taken for granted from the start?

I feel sorry for John Starks. In the six games of tit for tat with the (Houston) Rockets over the last two weeks, he has been one of the (New York) Knicks' better players. But tonight, in the deciding game of the best-of-seven series, he had a stinker, an absolute nightmare. The stats – two baskets from seventeen attempts – tell it all; it just wasn't happening for him around the net. Indeed, alongside Hakeem Olajuwon, he was the Rockets' most valuable asset. Which is crazy when you think about it. I mean, what was Pat Reilly, the Knicks' coach, thinking of? Recognised widely as the Jack Charlton of the basketball world, how on earth could he stand by and watch as Starks blew the game? If Jack *had* been in charge tonight, we'd have seen a very different John Starks, because if he hadn't been sorted out by the first quarter...

'John, it's not happening for you tonight. When you get up around the net, give it to someone else – use your loaf, man!'

...he most definitely would have been by the second.

'Right, get off! If you're not gonna do what I say, you're coming off.'

Or can't they make substitutions in basketball?

Anyway, for John (and for me because I had ten dollars on the Knicks with David Kelly) the game was one long nightmare. He was still trying – and missing – up until the final seconds of the game, and in the end the Rockets were six points too good. After eleven, when it was over, I suddenly felt quite peckish and immediately began canvassing in the communal room, where I'd been watching the game, for a bite of supper: 'Anyone fancy something to eat?'

Cass, John Sheridan, Denis and Kevin were playing cards. Dave Kelly and a couple of others were grouped around the telly.

'No thanks.'

'Naahh.'

'Not me.'

Disappointed at the poor response and driven by the growing pangs in my stomach, I tried again. 'Seriously? Not even a McDonald's, a milkshake?'

Cass was first to crack: 'Yeah, I'll have a milkshake.'

Then Shez: 'Yeah, go on. I'll have a milkshake.'

Encouraged by the rush on milkshakes and determined not to eat my Big Mac alone, I persisted. 'Nothing to eat... Cass? Anyone?'

'Oh go on,' Cass said. 'I'll have a quarter-pounder with cheese.'

'Yeah, I'll have one of them.'

'A McChicken sandwich.'

'Big Mac for me,' until at last we had an order. Handed a fistful of dollars, Mick went down to reception and organised a taxi – 'MacMeals on MacWheels' if you like. And twenty minutes later we were all slurping from our shakes and biting into burgers.... Funny, but it tasted really great at the time. But not now. Not forty minutes later. It's midnight and as the ketchup, gherkins, onions, beef, cheese, bun and chocolate (shake) begin to fuse, there are new pangs in my stomach. And I'm wishing I hadn't. I'm most definitely wishing I hadn't!

DAY 18

THURSDAY JUNE 23:

SOD'S LAW

After thirty minutes on the training ground, Millwall's manager returned to the locker-room in a dishevelled state. Sweat dripping from the bridge of his nose, he said, 'All the best tomorrow you lot – you'll need it. It was so hot out there I was breathing out of my arse.' I have always liked and admired Mick McCarthy. An excellent skipper whose trenchant honesty in the dressing-room occasionally rubbed one or two up the wrong way, he was fired by an intense competitive spirit and was driven by a fierce commitment to the team. When his voice boomed around Lansdowne Road, didn't you know it! Things are a lot quieter when we play there these days. It doesn't surprise me that he is doing well at Millwall, for he is real management material, a good talker and knows what he wants from a team. He seemed in good spirits at the training ground this morning. I'm looking forward to sitting down with him over a beer after the game.

The game. We've hardly even thought about it since Italy last week. We didn't do much at training – a few stretches, a couple of jogs across the pitch, and while those who didn't play on Saturday were given a more vigorous work-out, for the rest it was: 'That's enough, get off, get out of the sun. Go and sit in the shade or on the bus, or go back to the dressing-room, but go now. Get off this training ground.' After a shower and a change, we returned to the hotel and were summoned to watch the video of Sunday's Norway-Mexico game. We all hate the videos – such a drag. Especially a game like this, when you know the Norwegians score in the eighty-fifth minute. Much more fun to watch it live. But it's part of the job, so we sat and studied and yawned our way through. Mexico, though they lost, looked the better team, but it just wouldn't drop for them – and how they didn't score in the goal-mouth scramble right at the end, I will never know. The fella's headed from three yards into an open goal... it's come off the post... he's two yards closer... it hits him on the head again – and somehow goes over the post. Incredible!

When it was over, Jack took out his notes. 'Right, you've had a little look at them. The big fella out on the left is a good runner with the ball – watch him, he's useful. Sanchez is looking to link with other players. The number ten in midfield, Garcia, is a useful player, but they don't like crosses whipped in at them and they won't like you going at them. I've some more things to say about them, but we'll talk again tonight after dinner.' And with that, we shot back to our rooms to watch Italy playing Norway.

'This is going to be a long, long afternoon for the Norwegians,' Jack's son John said after fifteen minutes of the game. 'I can see Italy giving them a right hammering.' The game started at great pace. Italy looked a different team to the one we beat on Saturday and seemed clearly intent on business. But then, just when it looked as if they would give the Norwegians a roasting, Franco Baresi got it wrong with his favourite tool. As he charged out to play the off-side trap, with Maldini and Costacurta – his team-mates at Milan – alongside, the right back Benarrivo (who plays for Parma and isn't as tuned to Baresi's ways) stayed in playing the onrushing Leonhardsen on-side. Reacting to the danger, Pagliuca immediately raced from his goal, spread himself at Leonhardsen's feet and diverted the Norwegian's attempt to round him with his hand, well outside his box. He was immediately sent off and our attention now turned to the Italian bench, where an animated Sacchi was giving it the old '*Mamma Mia*'. Pagliuca's red card meant he had to put on Marchegiani, the number two keeper – but who was he going to take off? The substitution boards went up, Marchegiani ran on and, to everyone's surprise, Roberto Baggio, the main man, was asked to pay the tab.

At first it seemed a crazy decision, but playing with great heart and spirit, Dino Baggio headed them in front with twenty minutes to go and they held on, deservedly winning the match. Norway, it must be said, were absolute crap – played with no bottle at all. If they had gone for Italy's throat they could have knocked them out of the tournament, instead of gutlessly settling for a draw when Italy were down to ten men. In the end they, too, got what they deserved.

The mood in the camp is good – as calm and relaxed as it was before the Italian game. And yet there is something about this game, an unease I feel that leaves me... not worried but a bit concerned. The result this afternoon hasn't helped. While I was pleased to see them win, 1–0 to Italy was the last result we wanted because, although on the one hand it has left us in pole position in the group, the race, as Damon Hill will confirm, is never over until you pass the chequered flag. Yes, we are in a strong position, but unless we can follow the performance against Italy with another one tomorrow, then it will count for nothing. Worse! If we were to lose 1–0, each of the four teams will have played, won and lost by exactly the same margin – sending us back to square one with one game to play. Not that I believe we will be beaten tomorrow. We should get something out of it, but it will be tougher than people think.

As a team, you see, because of the size of the country and the small pool of players available to the team, we have always felt comfortable in the role of the underdog. As underdogs, we can approach a game like Saturday's feeling calm and relaxed, because ultimately we can't lose. We were 'David' and Italy were 'Goliath', a class team. Which brings me to the source of my unease. Because of Saturday's result and the way we've played in the warm-up games, tomorrow we are Goliath. We're the class side, expected to win – which would be fair enough if the game was being played in the cool of an evening in Europe. But it's not, is it? It's being played in Orlando – not exactly Mexico's back yard but pretty close. Will we be able to compete in the heat for ninety minutes? I'm not sure. The forecast is for 95 degrees with 65 per cent humidity, but as I look out the window tonight, I'm hoping for the morning showers that were a feature of our first few days here. Not that I believe we will get them. It's Sod's Law isn't it? Tomorrow will be a scorcher.

DAY 19

FRIDAY JUNE 24:
SOME LIKE IT HOT

08:15   Sod's Law. That little gap in the curtains – you can always tell, it never lies. I'm not even going to look. Typical, bloody typical.

08:30   Breakfast – cereal, a couple of bits of toast – I'm not that hungry. Jackie and the kids are out in the lobby. I give them their tickets, then head up to the room and put my feet up.

09:45   Channel surfing, I come across a live report from the Citrus Bowl on the local news station. With temperatures running higher than expected, a guy with a microphone standing in the middle of the pitch announces dramatically (everything on TV here is theatre) that playing conditions are expected to top 110 degrees – exactly what I don't want to hear. The injustice of it all is already beginning to grate. 'Is it fair that we should have to play here and Norway and Italy don't? Is it right that we should have to face a South American team in South American temperatures when two of our rivals don't? Surely the idea of a group is that conditions for each team are the same? Okay, so Norway come down and it rains, but we could live with that. I don't know, it just doesn't seem fair.

10:15   Mick gives us the call to head down to the bus. Because of the early kick-off, the traditional day-of-the-match stroll is abandoned. On the way to the ground, I sit with Aldo down the back. 'I've got bad vibes about this game today,' he says in his thick scouse accent. 'I've got bad vibes... this heat, it worries me.'
   'Yeah, it will be murder,' Ronnie agrees.

10:45   As soon as we arrive at the ground, we walk out to inspect the pitch. It's boiling hot, but the good news is that there is a breeze. The bad news is that it has blown straight from the Sahara desert. Stan, who is very fair skinned and really struggles in the heat, is worried whether he will last a game. I'm feeling a bit heavy-legged myself.

11:00 'This is going to be a very tough game for you today,' Jack says when we return to the dressing-room. He talks a little about the Mexicans, gives us our instructions for the game and then, almost as an afterthought, laughs: 'Oh, by the way – same team.' The card school break out a deck. We sit around, watch TV. The mood is reasonably upbeat. With half an hour to go, I begin to get ready. Charlie distributes the kit – white. 'Are you sure about this Charlie?'

12:30 As we walk out, my first thoughts are for Daniel and Kelly. I told Jackie to take hats and sun-block, but the heat's so intense I wonder if they'll suffer. We line up for the anthems – they seem to last for ever – then exchange pennants, and with a blast from the referee's whistle the game gets under way. It starts well for us. Stan plays a great ball to Terry Phelan, who has gone sprinting down the left on an over-lapping run. Terry whips a lovely ball across for Tommy Coyne, who would definitely have put it away if the bounce had been kinder.

12:45 We're still looking for it. The early goal. Score first and it will be like a cool breeze on our foreheads – put that extra bit of spring in our step, give us something to hang on to. But the ball won't bounce for us. It won't bounce for me. Thirty-three minutes gone, we win a touch deep in their half. Terry throws it long for Tommy, who flicks into their box for me to run on to. Racing to the bounce, I pause for the ball to come off the floor so I can hit it. Or head it... yes, I'll head it, I'm sure the bounce will be high. But the bounce is low. Too late for me to redistribute my weight, I lunge at it with my head – but knock it down and off my hand. Campos dives... ohhh... just manages to turn it around. If only I had read the bounce, I could have buried it with my foot.

13:13 Two minutes to go to half-time: rest and refreshment await. Mexico are on the attack. Del Olmo cuts inside Terry Phelan, squares the ball to Luis Garcia... Garcia shoots from twenty-five yards, low and hard to Packie's right. Garcia scores! One–nil to Mexico. A cruel blow that punishes us for the possession we have carelessly conceded in the half.

13:20 The dressing-room is like the first-aid tent in a war zone. It's not easy being captain when the ship has just been hit. Sitting with an ice pack and a towel around my head, I'm not sure how inspirational I sound when I stand up to say my few words: 'Lads, let's make sure we don't concede any more. We'll get a chance or two. Let's stick together now.' Jack is philosophical. The heat, the conditions... we are a long, long way from what we're used to at Lansdowne Road. 'We've got to do it better than the way we are now,' he urges. 'If someone goes, he must be backed up by someone else. It's no good someone going on his own, because he'll just be picked off with passes; you've got to support each other and take the game to them now. Don't panic, keep going and *don't* concede any more. If it's not going to happen for us today, then it is going to end 1–0, but we are not going to concede any more.'

Then, searching out Steve Staunton, he continues: 'Are you all right, Stan? You look knackered. Just give me another ten or fifteen minutes and I'll pull you off.... Tommy! Same for you. Don't hold nothing back and then we'll make a change or two.'

13:30 Conscious of the errors of the opening half, we try to keep hold of the ball more, and for twenty minutes manage quite well. Roy sends John (Sheridan) in behind their last defender – a chance he would put away eight times out of ten, but the ball just runs away from him and he fails to take hold of the shot. A goal at that point would have been such a lift for us, but instead Garcia scores again and sends us crashing to the floor.

13:51 The playing field is a lonely place to be in moments like that. Although you are surrounded by thousands of people, although there are millions looking in, that walk with the ball to the centre circle can often be the loneliest walk in the world. 'Come on lads, we've got to dig in deep and hang in there,' I urge. Beaten though we look, throwing in the towel isn't an option. The boards go up on the touchline. Stan comes off, Ray switches to the left and Jason, whose enthusiasm for the game is proving a real shot in the arm, slots into Ray's position on the right. Aldo then warms up to replace Tommy Coyne, but just as he is about to run on, an official grabs him and starts pushing him about, ordering him to wait. Furious, Aldo is an iota away from – in his own words later – 'sparking' the guy and doesn't need to raise his adrenalin when eventually he's allowed on.

14:09 The goal, when it comes, is no more than we deserve. A great ball in from Jason – and if I had to choose any player in the world to be on the end of it, I would have chosen Aldo, the man who is. At thirty-five years old, Aldo's hunger for success and goals seems as sharp as it ever was. It's a brilliantly taken header from the goal-poacher supreme. Six minutes to go, we are suddenly back in the game.

14:11 Four minutes to go and the ball drops beautifully for me on the edge of their box. This time there are no mistakes. I hit as I want to hit it – high and hard towards the top left-hand corner of the net. For a split second I watch, expecting to see it ripple, but Campos, for all his daft shirts, is an agile keeper and he makes a good save. The final whistle blows. We walk from the field. It just didn't happen for me today. I feel like John Starks.

14:35 At first the mood is one of deep disappointment. We shower and change, too shattered to search for excuses or point the finger, but Jack gives us all a lift when he returns from his round of interviews. 'I'm very proud of the effort you've put in here today. I couldn't have asked for any more – in the end you almost ran the legs off them. They were dead on their feet, and another five minutes and you would probably have got one. But,' he continues, 'don't worry. That goal could be like a point to us Aldo – great finish. We're not ready to go home yet.'

15:45 We return by bus to the Hilton, where the FAI (to their credit) have arranged a buffet for the players' immediate family and friends. Not that hungry, I eat a bowl of soup and chat to my brother Mike. Out in the lobby, the journalists are queueing for interviews to fit around their theories on how we lost the game. One of these is interesting enough. 'Would you agree,' I'm asked, 'that when you go into something expecting the worst, the worst inevitably happens?' Hmmm, deep one that – one for Jimmy Case. I think about it. 'Yes,' I reply. 'That does tend to happen in life… but the reason we lost the game? No, I'm not sure it's that simple. I believe it was a combination of things – the heat, the results of last weekend, the fact that they desperately needed a result after their defeat to Norway, the fact that we didn't need it quite as bad. I don't know.' It's interesting… one to reflect on beside the fire this winter, but not something I care to think about too deeply now.

20:00 Released from squad duties for the next twenty-four hours, we leave the hotel in Jackie's rented Chevvy and drive to the apartment in

Kissimee. It feels good to be away from the lads, good to be with your wife and kids under the same roof. Daniel and Kelly are exhausted. We put them to bed, open a beer and talk family – whether they should stay on now for the duration, or return to England as planned with Jackie's mum tomorrow. We decide to let them stay.

It's rare that we talk about football. During the early days at Southampton, there were times when she'd awake and find me sitting on the edge of the bed, worrying about how badly I had played and whether I'd be dropped from the team. At thirty-one, however, I'm no longer haunted by those sort of nightmares.

DAY 20

SATURDAY JUNE 25:
MOMENTS OF MADNESS

The night wasn't as peaceful as I would have wished. Kelly woke us with a call of nature at about five, and we were only just nodding off again when the phone rang with a wrong number. Jackie answered it at first... and again when it rang a second time twenty seconds later. But when it rang for a third time, I jumped up and informed the guy in no uncertain terms that he had reached the wrong abode. Leaving the phone off the hook, I returned to bed and slept fitfully until nine.

Jackie's mum cooked a good old fry-up for breakfast (home, sweet home), then she packed her cases and we drove her to the airport for her flight back to London. While at the airport, we also made arrangements for the kids to stay on. With the team flying to New York tomorrow, we booked two additional seats on an American Airlines flight via Miami that Jackie had reserved for herself, Joanne (McGuinness) and Sarah (Cascarino). Stan and Joanne were at the apartment when we returned – or rather Joanne was. Stan had chosen a bed and was taking an afternoon nap. The heat continues to slaughter him. Three weeks of acclimatisation and he is still finding it very tough. His dad is suffering, too, and is getting restless sitting around the hotel. He'd like to be able to go for walk, but how do you go for a walk or take a breath of fresh air in Florida?

Stan's forty winks complete, we went for a meal to a pasta house up the road, Little Italy, then took the kids to a go-kart track before returning to the apartment at nine. The hour that followed was the most enjoyable of the day. We opened a beer, then another... talked about the season, how long and hard it had been... the Mexican game, how hot and hard it had been... the Norway game, how dogged and hard it would be... and both agreed that we wouldn't take much convincing to toss our boots aside.

'Do you know where I'd most like to be at this moment in time?' he asked. 'Sitting in me local with me mates in Dundalk.'

'It's funny you should say that,' I replied, surprised at the telepathy. 'I'm ready just to lie on a sun-bed and become a slob for a week or two. It's crazy, isn't it? You sweat for two years and bust a gut trying to get out here, and then you have moments of madness like this when you wish you were some place else.'

Ten o'clock. The curfew was drawing near. 'Don't keep looking at your watch', Jackie complained, suspicious we were plotting a last beer in town. But for once our motives were genuine. At a quarter to eleven, we called a cab to take us back to the hotel. Stan's dad was sitting in the lobby as we arrived and I left them together, continuing on to the lift.

Jack's door was ajar as I walked towards my room. 'Come in,' he shouted as I went past. Frank Gillespie and Maurice Setters were with him. I stood in the doorway, declined the offer of a glass of stout, and listened as he told me about the fine (20,000 Swiss francs) and touch-line ban that had been imposed on him after the palaver over Aldo's substitution the day before. 'I want you to organise a whip-round among the lads,' he laughed. He didn't seem too upset.

Mick's door was also ajar when I went past. Explaining that I wasn't happy with the travelling arrangements Jackie had made for New York (a five o'clock flight to Miami meant that they wouldn't touch down in Newark until late on Sunday night), I asked if he could see Donie Butler (the commercial manager of the FAI) about the possibility of squeezing them on to the team flight, which was direct and leaving at noon.

'If there are seats available,' I asked him, 'knock me up half an hour before everyone else, because Kissimee is a forty-minute drive and she is going to need the extra time to get organised and over here.' As he agreed he would see what he could do, I thanked him and went to bed.

Manhattan transfers

Norway
(June 26 to June 29)

SUNDAY JUNE 26:

BEHIND EVERY GOOD MAN...

Mick rapped on the door at eight. 'It's done,' he said. 'Donie says there are five seats.'

'Oh cheers, Mick.' I raced straight to the phone.

'Jackie! Are you packed – are you ready?'

'Well, not exactly. Why?'

'Mick says there are seats on the plane, but you have to be at the hotel by 9:30 because the buses leave here at 9:45.'

'Oh great – but what about the car we've hired?'

'Forget that, just drive it over here. I'll make up some fantastic lie and they can pick it up at the hotel. But hurry, you don't have much time.'

Working out how long it would take her to get the kids ready and thinking about the length of the journey across, I worried they would be cutting it fine. Fortunately, however, this being a Sunday morning, traffic on Interstate 4 was light and they arrived bang on time. Well pleased that we would be travelling to New York together, I didn't even groan when they announced that our flight was delayed.

On the flight I sat next to Mick and Charlie, with Jackie, Daniel and Kelly a few rows back. Kelly couldn't understand why her Daddy wasn't sitting with them, and too young, at the age of four, to grasp team protocol, she kept standing on her seat and asking, 'Are you all right, Daddy?' from behind.

The arrangements for New York were the same as before the Italian game, and at Newark airport there was a bus waiting on the Tarmac to take us direct to the Tara Sheraton. Once installed in our rooms, we changed and prepared to go training in the evening at local University grounds. It felt great to run off the aches and pains of Friday and, over-all, the session was one of the sharpest we've had. Nothing focuses the mind quite like defeat, and although our next game was two days away, already we were all looking forward to it.

It was near enough 8:30 when we got back to the hotel. I was standing in the lobby, waiting for the lift, when out of the blue Jack said: 'Is that your missus over there?' Aware that the wives had booked into the team hotel, I knew, before even turning around, that it was. I also knew, from the edge in Jack's voice, that he wasn't pleased about it. Feigning surprise, I walked over to Jackie, who was standing across the lobby near some phones. 'He's seen you here,' I said, before she could say a word.

'Oh, I'm sorry,' she said. 'We were just going for something to eat. I didn't expect you'd be back quite so soon.'

'It's okay, don't worry about it. I'll say you tried to get into the Hilton but it was fully booked.'

Taking a deep breath, I turned back and prepared my excuse for Jack, but as I approached he suddenly lost his head. 'What the hell are you doing? I'm talking here and you lot are earwigging – that's out of order,' he yelled at a cameraman, who had just zoomed in on a private conversation he was having with a couple of the lads. Jackie, standing twenty yards away, thought he was having a go at me. 'My legs were trembling,' she told me later. 'If he had come over to me, I'd have just burst into tears.'

Returning to the room I sought Cass' advice. 'Cass, he's just seen Jackie downstairs. What am I gonna say?'

But Cass wasn't much help – 'Oh well, I don't know' – so I decided to go and knock on Jack's door.

'Jack, they [Jackie, Joanne, Sarah and Caroline McGrath] tried to get in across the road, but it was fully booked – they've nowhere else to go. We won't have anything whatsoever to do with them until after the game.'

He looked at me, put his head to one side and said, 'Fair enough then, okay.' Walking away, I felt relieved he had accepted my explanation, but I also felt annoyed that I should have to bend the truth. I completely understand Jack's stance; indeed, until recently I would have agreed with it. Relationships can be minefields. Wives can upset the balance of a closely woven team, so why expose your team to a hazard you can easily cut out? If only it were as simple as that, but this is not your normal mid-week international. These are the World Cup finals we are talking about here – the greatest show on earth. Is it fair to expect players' wives and children to sit and watch it on TV? And given that some are going to want to travel anyway, surely it would make more sense and alleviate a lot of worry if they were pencilled into the itinerary from the very start. Will my performance suffer on

Tuesday because my wife has spent the last two nights sleeping four floors beneath me? I think not. I mean, just because they are staying in the same hotel doesn't mean they have to interfere. Jackie wouldn't dream of it. She doesn't want to come to the training ground every day. She doesn't expect me to sit down and have dinner with her or play with the kids in the pool. Aware of the rules and the demands that have been placed upon me, she just wants to be near, to participate without taking part.

'I've told Sarah to keep out of the way,' Cass said when I returned to the room.

'No,' I replied, 'that's wrong. We shouldn't have to tell them to keep out of the bloody way.'

'Naaah, but you know what I mean.'

'Yes, I do know what you mean, but the more I think about it, the more I think it's wrong. We shouldn't have to tell our wives, "Don't be in reception at nine o'clock, that's when we come down to breakfast." We shouldn't have to say, "Make sure you're not near the lift at seven because we might be coming up in it." That's wrong.'

At the dinner table, Phil Babb recommended we watch *House Party* tonight, but when we returned to our room and tuned in, we couldn't make head nor tail of it – neither me or Cass. Full of back-slapping and high fives and all this coloured street talk, it wasn't just bad, it was deplorably bad.

'Phil has absolutely done us here,' said Cass, 'done us like a kipper.'

Switching channels, I decided to watch *The Krays* instead. Hey! That was more like it – the kind of street talk me and Cass understand. But Cass was tired and, turning into his pillow, tried to get some sleep – not that easy with all those bullets flying around.

'Is there any danger of us getting some sleep tonight?' he asked.

'Fair enough,' I replied, and turned out the light.

# DAY 22

MONDAY JUNE 27:

PAUL MCGRATH... OHHH, AHHH

Jack pulled me at training this morning. 'I'm a bit undecided about whether to play Paul tomorrow. What do you think?' Surprised that he should consult me, I didn't feel comfortable as I tried to compose my reply. While we all have opinions about who should play, I tend to keep my opinions to myself, (a) because I wouldn't like to offend any of my team-mates and (b) because... well, maybe there is no (b). It's not that I'm afraid to voice my opinion, just that I don't believe it is my job, my place. And besides, Jack is so set in his ways that when he asks your opinion, I'm not sure he is all that interested in your reply a lot of the time. Clearly unhappy with Paul's performance in the Mexican game, he was obviously thinking strongly of leaving him out. I didn't agree.

'Tomorrow will be a completely different game to the one we played in the other day. They'll sling a lot of stuff into the box in the air, and although I've only played with him for a season at Villa, I know enough about him to know that when he is on his game – no matter how big they are – he'll head it, he'll get above them. But if you're worried about him, then go and speak with him and lay it on the line. I guarantee he won't let you down; I'd put my house on him. But that's only my opinion – it's your decision.'

'Okay,' he said, and I trotted back to the pack. Later, I noticed him having a word with Paul, but when I quizzed Paul about it, he just said Jack was going to sleep on it and would make a decision in the morning.

The group has gone down to the wire. Tomorrow, at the same time as we kick off against Norway in the Giants Stadium, Italy kick off against Mexico in Washington DC. These are the permutations: while a win will guarantee us a place in the next round and defeat will see us eliminated, John Aldridge's goal against Mexico means that a draw (superior goals scored) will also be good enough. That leaves us in a difficult situation. Do we play to win or to draw? I spoke to Kevin this morning about it and he's in absolutely no doubt.

'We need to get everybody's mind focused on winning tomorrow,' he said, 'not on protecting. We must make sure now that there's no talk of "If we draw that will put us second or third, which means we'll have to play so-and-so in such-and-such a city." Let there be none of that. It's quite clear: we win the match tomorrow and our destiny is in our own hands. We will stay in New York where the conditions suit us – and that has to be what we aim for.'

He's right, of course, but will Jack look on it like that? I'm not sure. Jack is very tactically minded, won't want to state categorically, 'Go out and win the game,' in case we commit hara-kiri along the way and end up losing it when a draw would have done. In a way, the situation we find ourselves in is not too dissimilar to our last qualifying game against Northern Ireland last November. Although back then, of course, there were other elements involved....

On a blustery night in Belfast

While playing for the Republic these last five years has heightened my awareness of things Irish, when we flew to Belfast on the afternoon of November 16 last year, I was landing in a city whose complexities I didn't know a great deal about. A week before the game, ten people had died in a bombing on the Shankill Road and seven had been shot dead while enjoying Saturday night drinks in a pub in County Derry. With tensions running high, there was all sorts of speculation that the game would be switched to a neutral venue in England, and when eventually it was decided to progress as planned, the phone never stopped ringing.

'Are the players secretly worried about their safety next week?' reporters asked.

'Look,' I replied, keen to play it down, 'this is an international football match, the final game in the qualifying series for the World Cup finals in America – nothing more. The players are not worried about their safety, just concerned, in the way that everybody is concerned, about the recent developments there.'

Privately, however, we were all a bit more concerned than we were admitting – not just for ourselves, but for our supporters, who would inevitably ignore official advice and travel up to the game.

The camera crews and reporters were out in force when we touched down.

'Jack? How do you feel about having to play the game in Belfast?'

'No problem,' said Jack as he continued to walk past. Now Jack actually wanted the game to be played at Windsor Park; he wanted the 'North' – urged on by their support – to come on to us, as this would greatly facilitate our task. 'I'll be all right either way,' he joked. 'I'll just put me arm around Billy [Bingham, the Northern Ireland manager]. I'm a Protestant.'

Religion reared its head again in the lead-up, with people discussing the number of Catholics on the Northern Ireland team, the number of Protestants who played for the Republic. It always does whenever we meet. I can never understand that – what the hell does it matter? Okay, I know all about tradition and I appreciate people's beliefs, but when it comes to sport and entertainment (and, although it's probably not obvious to those who watch me every week, football is in there somewhere), should we have been talking religious divide?

The first time we saw guns was on the morning of the game. A golf course behind the hotel was a nice setting for the pre-match stroll... until we noticed these soldiers with machine guns just off a fairway. They weren't exactly searching for balls in the rough, and I remember looking at them and wondering about the risks they were taking and how on earth they could do it for a living – a question I had put to one of our RUC (Royal Ulster Constabulary) minders on the way to training at Windsor Park the evening before. He was a very friendly fellow, and I began by asking him about the ground and the type of area it was in (loyalist) and if there had been any problems with our visit. Then I moved on to what interested me most: why he would work in a job where he was a terrorist target every day.

'I wouldn't do it if it didn't pay well,' he replied. 'No way. It gives me a better lifestyle than a lot of other jobs.'

Listening to him talk about the job and its problems was fascinating, and I was struck by how little I know about the complexities of living here.

'Don't think that life in Northern Ireland is all bad news,' he stressed. But I was already reaching that conclusion. The hotel staff and the security people looking after us were smashing, couldn't have been nicer. Indeed, in the day and a half we spent there, we encountered no animosity at all. Not, that is, until it was time to walk out for the game.

People shout at you all the time in football – it's part and parcel of watching from the terraces. A week before the Northern Ireland game, we (Aston Villa) were away to Arsenal at Highbury when, in the dying minutes, an irate 'Gunner' (who obviously knew his football facts) roared: 'Hey, Townsend! Show us your medals.' (Four months later, I am happy to report, this anomaly was rectified in the League Cup final.) To score a minute later was the perfect answer. Running back to where he was sitting, I gave him a thumbs up and a smile – much to the amusement of his mates.

Twelve days later, however, as I led out the Republic of Ireland in that last World Cup qualifier at Windsor Park, a very different breed of supporter shouted my name. More hateful than anything I had heard before, he screamed: 'Hey Townsend, you fucking English bastard. I hope your mother dies of cancer.' Instantly taken aback, I wondered what exactly we were getting into. I mean, I had played in all sorts of intimidating venues before – the Olympic Stadium in Rome in the World Cup quarter-finals, the away qualifiers against Spain and Denmark in Seville and Copenhagen – but this was different, very different. With only 10,000 people in the ground, it was what they were saying rather than the volume they were saying it at.

It being a bitterly cold evening with a swirling wind, we didn't warm up for long before the game. As I tapped the ball around, I noticed Billy Bingham pointing towards us and then gesturing to the crowd. It was more than a simple, 'Let's hear it for the boys' solicitation; he was motioning with his hand, whipping up the support up as if to say, 'Come on, let's remind them where they are. Let's get at their throats.' That surprised me, because although I had never had much to do with him before, Bingham had always struck me as an amiable man, the 'father-figure' type who never appeared ruffled. His antagonism towards our team in the build-up had also surprised me; for him to have accused our players of being mercenaries who only played for Ireland because they weren't good enough for England and Scotland was untrue, unfair and not very clever, given the political temperature at the time. 'Play with your heads, not your hearts,' Jack warned, before we ran out. But that was easier said than done, and by the end of the night, even he would get carried away with what was pumping hard inside.

Our task was clear enough: to be sure of qualifying we needed to win – or draw if the game in Seville between Spain and Denmark ended with a decisive result. Opting to start against the wind, we opened cautiously and tried to play it tight. Full of running and driven by 'heart', they came at us and were much the better side when we walked in at the interval. In the dressing-room, the news from Seville was bad: 0–0 at half-time; Spain had had their goalkeeper sent off and were down to ten men. Jack laid it on the line: 'Spain have had their keeper sent off and are probably going to be happy to play for a draw in the hope that we draw. Winning is going to be a tall order for them now with ten men, so if we want to make sure, we are going to have to win.' I can remember there was no sense of panic as we listened to his words; with forty-five minutes to play, the wind in our tails would change the gradient of the slope. Walking back out, we were sure the game would turn. It did... but not in the way we had expected.

There is nothing more desperate in football than being a goal away from the World Cup finals. We were moving forward with new urgency, but try as we did, the goal wouldn't come. Then, in the sixty-third minute, we got word from the bench that Spain had gone one up in Seville. 'Shit,' I thought. 'A draw might just be enough.' We pressed on, caught between two stools, the urgency of needing to win diluted by a heightened caution of defeat. For ten minutes we walked this delicate line until, totally against the run of play, Jimmy Quinn smacked a volley into the roof of our net. We were stunned. I mean, sometimes you can feel a goal coming, sometimes you are being so worn down that it comes as no surprise – but this was totally out of the blue. The sixty seconds that followed were numbing. A two-year voyage via Copenhagen, Seville, Tirana, Riga and Vilnius seemed set to end in Belfast and not the United States as planned. In those few seconds I felt low, so low, lower than a snake's belly.

Cass remembers the second half more vividly than most. With the game still finely balanced at nil–nil, Jack wasn't just boiling, he was positively steaming, with most of his wrath directed at Ray (Houghton) who, playing on the left, was closest to the bench. Standing at the edge of the dug-out, he would turn around to Cass whenever Ray made a mistake and, hands on cap, roar: '*Look at him! Look at fucking Raymond!*' And Cass would shuffle his feet and try to look the other way. The minutes ticked on, Jack wound tighter, and when Ray tried something that didn't quite come off he completely lost his head. '*Off, get him off,*' he roared at Cass. And Cass sort of looked at him, stunned. He said it again: '*Get him fucking off!*' Twenty minutes of the second half had passed when the boards came out. Alan (McLoughlin) ran on and Jimmy Quinn scored to leave us 1–0 down.

Immediately after Quinn's goal, Jack turned to Cass again and told him to get stripped, that he was going on. Now poor Cass, it must be explained, had been having a terrible run of luck. Hammered every night at cards, he had been awarded the dreaded yellow bib for the worst player in the five-a-side on the eve of the game. Given the nod by Jack, however, he felt the run looked set to change. Ripping off his coat and track suit with great enthusiasm and vigour, he couldn't believe it when he found that all he had under it was a white Adidas T-shirt. He had left his playing shirt on the peg in the dressing-room! Jack, meanwhile, was getting edgy – 'Come on, get a move on' – until it dawned on him why it was that Cass was so slow.

'Where's your bloody shirt?' he screamed in disbelief.

'I've left it in the dressing-room,' a stricken Cass replied.

'Whaaat! You fucking idiot!' Jack turned to Charlie O'Leary: 'Charlie! Sprint in and get his shirt.' But Cass had his own ideas on how to retrieve the situation. Turning to Dave Kelly, he asked him to loan him his shirt – but this only made matters worse.

'You can't bloody well do that,' Jack roared. 'You'll have us thrown out of the fucking tournament, you idiot. Charlie....' So with that, Charlie sprinted off in the direction of the dressing-room and as he did, Cass envisaged the ultimate nightmare of the room being locked, with the key in the pocket of some old geezer in the stand. Happily, however, his fears proved unfounded and as soon as Charlie returned, Cass discarded his T-shirt and was ready to run on. Meanwhile out on the field, events were taking a fresh turn.

At exactly the same moment as Cass slipped on his shirt, Eddie McGoldrick was fouled when attacking near their corner flag. Denis Irwin stepped up to take the free kick and his floated cross was nodded down straight on to the chest of an attentive Alan McLoughlin, who volleyed the ball straight into the back of their net. One–all in Belfast, one–nil in Seville – with fourteen minutes to play, we were suddenly on course again.

With five minutes to go, I remember glancing across and being struck by how calm everyone seemed. Had Denmark equalised? Was the link with Seville and the news of a Spanish goal just a wind-up? I wasn't sure. Mick wasn't his usual cat-on-a-hot-tin-roof self and the others all had their hands in their pockets, apparently lacking that habitual frantic anxiousness.

When the referee blew for time, David Kelly was first across with the news. 'That's it, it's all over,' he shouted excitedly. 'Spain have won 1–0.' And with that he gave me a hug. Roy Keane came over and joined in, and in the space of thirty seconds the pitch was transformed into one giant merry-go-round. Mick was already shedding tears and Packie had gone as white as a sheet, drained by the emotional swings of the night and relieved it had all come good. Alan McDonald, the Northern Ireland captain, then came over and congratulated me. 'I hope you have a great summer,' he said. I appreciated the gesture, knew it was sincere, and those moments out on the pitch were absolutely brilliant... until I reached the ramp to the dressing-room and Sean Connolly informed me they were still at it in Seville. 'You're joking,' I gasped in disbelief. 'You've got to be... we've just been... every photographer in the world caught us beaming from ear to ear.'

By the time I reached the dressing-room, confirmation came through that the game had indeed ended 1–0 to Spain, and the celebrations resumed. Not that we were feeling in any way euphoric. No, it was more a sense of relief than anything else. Jack being Jack, he came in and told us we had all played crap. He had really wanted us to win the game, wanted it badly, but he loosened out as the night went on and the results of the other groups began to filter through.

Leaving the ground immediately after the game, we drove straight to the airport for a flight back to Dublin. Although it was one o'clock in the morning when we touched down, the reception was unbelievable. Stepping off the plane, I felt like one of the Beatles – there were television cameras and microphones everywhere and a huge crowd of cheering people. That we had been disappointing on the night no longer mattered. The essential had been secured. England, Scotland, Wales and Northern Ireland hadn't made it, but we had. We were going to the USA.

 **DAY 23**

TUESDAY JUNE 28:
'JACK CALLING MAURICE'

08:00   The vibes are good. This is not a game I fear we will lose. Norway are not the unknown danger that Mexico were; we play against most of them every week, and man for man we are the better team. The only fear I have about them is in the set-piece. They're a bit like Wimbledon – capable of scoring goals not through individual flair or a flash of brilliance, but *à la* Fashanu from a corner, free kick or long throw. I must admit, they've done well to reach the finals: to take three points each off England and Holland was no mean feat, but England, it must be said, were a confused team in the latter days of Graham Taylor's reign and Norway couldn't have chosen a better time to play them. I'm not sure if they've really progressed since, and I was amazed at the tactics they employed against Italy on Thursday. A man to the good, they failed to capitalise, and showed real weakness in trying to play safe – a weakness we are confident we can exploit.

08:30   You don't change a winning breakfast; scrambled egg had been good enough for Italy and it would be good enough for Norway as well. As I return to the room, the rash starts to flare up again. It couldn't be the eggs... could it?

10:15   Mick raps on the door: 'The green machine is on the move again.' We descend to the bus, drive to the ground and are surprised when we are pointed towards the dressing-room the Italians used last time. We sit down, choose a locker and are talking amongst ourselves when I notice Jack approach.

'Paul, can I have a word?' My first thoughts are that he isn't going to play him, because I've seen it happen so many times at club level – the old arm around the shoulder and then, 'Sorry, son. I'm leaving you out.' When they return three or four minutes later, Jack calls us together to announce the team. Packie, Gary Kelly (in at right back for the suspended Denis Irwin), Stan (at left back for the suspended Terry

Phelan), Phil Babb, *Paul*, Jason, John, Roy, myself, Ray and Aldo up front.

He talks a bit about the Norwegians. 'You've seen enough of them, you're playing against them week in, week out. There is nothing hidden in there that I think we need to know about. What I will say, though, is that it's going to be a tough game. They will be as strong as you, as quick as you, as physically up for it as you – but I think you've got bigger hearts, and when push comes to shove, I think you'll be standing in the end. But it will be a tough game. Concentrate for ninety minutes, use your heads and play sensibly – and don't be surprised if they come out and have a go early on, because they need to win.'

Maurice Setters then speaks about some of the comments Norwegian manager Egil Olsen has been making in the build-up. 'He's been predicting this is going to be a battle, a war. He's been saying that he doesn't particularly rate us, that we don't have any outstanding players....'

'True,' Jack interrupts. 'He's got a point there, it's true – but we've got eleven bloody good ones.'

11:45   In order to overcome the handicap of his touchline ban, Jack will communicate his instructions to Maurice via a walkie-talkie from his seat in the stand. Joe Delaney wires each of them up with an ear piece and a microphone and they test them while standing barely two feet apart.

'Hello... Maurice... Maurice can you hear me?'

'All right. Yeah, yeah. I can hear that.'

Now the thought of Jack screaming into this thing while he's sitting somewhere in the stands is mind-boggling. Can you picture it? One of the lads losing possession, Jack turning to the Norwegian beside him with the paint on his face and the horns on his head, and screaming blue murder. What will the poor supporter think?

12:15   Shin pads on, rings taped, boots tied, ready. As we line out side by side, the atmosphere in the tunnel is slightly different from our two previous games. Against the Mexicans, I could have turned around and said, 'Let's get stuck into this lot today and they won't fancy it one bit,' knowing they wouldn't have understood a word. But with five of the Norwegians playing in the English Premiership, the 'this-lot-are-shit-lads-if-we-get-at-them-they'll-crap-themselves' speech might easily backfire, so I face the front and don't say a word until the referee leads us out to the pitch. Conditions are perfect; although the temperature's still in the eighties, it feels almost like a cool evening in Birmingham during pre-season training.

12:30 The game starts well for us. 'Let's keep the bloody ball today,' John Sheridan urged before walking out, and for forty-five minutes we knock it around and dominate possession. But we just can't find a path to their goal. Content to let us come at them, they sit behind the ball. Their main tactic of hitting it from left back to right wing for Jostein Flo to attack the ball wasn't really working, (a) because Stan was doing a good job standing beneath him and (b) because Jason was getting to the left back so quick he hadn't the time to play anything incisive.

13:15 Walking in at half-time, I'm feeling a touch worried. Norway need to win, while a draw suits us fine – and yet for forty-five minutes they haven't attempted to come out and play. I tell Jack, 'It's making me edgy that they're not bloody bothering.' But he urges calm. 'It's okay, it's fine. I can understand the way you are feeling out there, but just keep concentrating.' Word filters through about the Italy-Mexico game: 0–0, a score-line that would have been fed to the other dressing-room as well. Forty-five minutes from elimination, Norway will surely now have to try.

13:35 Jason makes a mistake early in the second half. Defending as the Norwegians began to attack, he has done well to come back and dispossess one of their players and should put the ball into row 22 (no one has ever scored from there). Instead, in trying to beat his man, he loses it again, then compounds the error by conceding a free in a dangerous position. Ray's fuming and has a right go, but I urge him to be calm and say I'll have a word.

13:50 The first time I glance at the clock it says '65 minutes'. 'Great,' I think. 'Twenty-five more and we're there.' Sometimes, to look at a clock too early is a sign of panic, but sixty-five is nice; we're doing okay. Stirred at last from their slumber, the Norwegians are coming forward more. A ball drops into Soerloth in our box... he's about to shoot... I kick it just in time... but too late to avoid him toe-ending me right on the back of the knee. A minute later he catches me again – with his knee this time – in exactly the same place. Sore and stiff, the more I try to run, the more I realise I can no longer continue. And yet I don't want to go off. As captain, you feel like it's deserting a sinking ship. But this is no time for heroes, and with people of Ronnie's class waiting to come on, limping off isn't a problem. But sitting on the bench is.

14:00   The contrast between playing and spectating is startling. Out on the pitch I control my own destiny, but once I come off, I feel so helpless I might as well be sitting in the stands. Those last fifteen minutes are the longest of my life. I must have counted every one of them down – just like a bloody basketball match. They have a chance which bounces off our cross-bar. 'That's it,' one of the lads says. 'They'll never score now.' We have chances too. John is unlucky with a chip and Roy is unlucky with a half-chance he can't quite keep down. Joe Delaney keeps us informed of developments in the other game: 1–1 with five minutes to play. If both finish as they are, Mexico will top the group and stay in New York, we'll finish second and return to Orlando, Italy will finish third but have to hold their breath, and Norway will be eliminated.

14:15   When the final whistle blows, I'm not sure whether to laugh or cry. Delighted on the one hand to have achieved what we set out to achieve, on the other hand – having tasted the Giants Stadium – I'm gutted at the thought of having to return to the Citrus Bowl. Limping into the dressing-room, I put some ice on my knee straight away. 'Well done lads,' Jack says. 'It takes two teams to make a game, and they made it very hard for you today by not doing anything, but you've done very well to qualify out of this group.' Continuing, he goes on to talk about Orlando and the task ahead: 'But they won't fancy it any more than we do.' He is talking about Belgium. We all are....

15:15   After the fiasco of last time, a 'reception' at the dog track is the last place I want to go. We have been allotted six tickets each for access to this 'exclusive' lounge, and have been assured that it will be properly organised. However, it turns out to be bedlam, with what must be more than two thousand supporters in the hall. Searching through the mass of people for Jackie, I can't find her, and as soon as I sit down to rest my aching knee, I am besieged by requests for autographs. Now, as I've said before, I don't have a problem signing anything, but there is a time and place for it – and this isn't the time. Furious, I vent my frustration on the first FAI official I can find.

'Who the hell organised this?' I snap at the unfortunate Eddie Corcoran. 'We were given six tickets to give to people so we could have a bit of peace and quiet! What is going on?'

'It's nothing to do with me,' he says. 'What are you having a go at me for?'

'Well who is it to do with then? It's to do with someone from the Football Association. It's not right, it's not fair – the lads have just sweated their nuts off and they can't have a drink in peace.'

I'm still ranting when we return to the bus, but Cass has no sympathy for me.

'Serves you right, doesn't it?'

'What do you mean?'

'You knew full well what it was going to be like.'

'How do you mean?'

'It's always the same, isn't it? They were probably selling tickets on the door outside.'

16:30 Just before we return to the bus, one of the doormen informs me that my 'cousin is at the door'. Puzzled, I immediately think of Una, but when I go out, there's an older lady waiting, whose features seem vaguely familiar. Kit Browne, a daughter of my nan's brother Jackie, married Liam Brown from Mitchelstown in County Cork and emigrated to New York City, where they both run a restaurant called The Harbour Lights, near the Brooklyn Bridge.

'Do you know who I am?' she asks.

'Yes, yes I do,' I reply. (Now while her features do seem familiar, I actually don't know who she is, although I do remember hearing talk of her when Nell, her mother, died.)

I invite her inside, but we've only just begun talking when it's time for us to go. Handing me her phone number, she invites me to call at the restaurant if I get a chance. Aware that we'll have the day off tomorrow, I tell her I will.

17:00 When we get back to the hotel, we find that the FAI have arranged everything I'd been hoping for back at the dog track. They've laid on a lovely room that's spacious and relaxed, some nice food – we couldn't have asked for better. Which begs the question, why on earth couldn't we have come here straight after the game in the first place? I mean, I don't want to sound ungrateful or to appear over-critical of the

FAI, but they never cease to amaze me. They try to do things right – they try hard – but always manage to screw up. Basically, what they seem to lack is professionalism, an understanding of the game at the level we are playing it. A small analogy: they tie their boots up on match day and are just about to run out when their lace snaps. Shouldn't they have noticed it was frayed before running out? Or they run out on the pitch and slip arse-over-tit because their studs are too short. Shouldn't they have checked the surface of the pitch beforehand? Professionals don't make these mistakes. A bit of sensible forethought makes all the difference.

19:00   Larry Mullen organises a night in Manhattan for some of the lads, and though Jackie gives me the green light, I decide to hang on at the hotel. Tense and tetchy after the game, I loosen out a bit as the night wears on, have a few beers with Kevin and his wife Eleanor, and nip off to bed at two in the morning when a GMTV lady asks Jackie and me if we would talk live to the English nation on breakfast TV.

'If you don't mind, I'd rather not,' I insist. 'I might fall off the chair.'

DAY 24

WEDNESDAY JUNE 29:

MANHATTAN TRANSFERS

Having been reunited with Jackie and the kids for the night, I got up at nine thirty, gave Daniel and Kelly a bath and went down for breakfast at ten. A bus was organised to take a group of us – fifteen adults and eight kids – into Manhattan. Separating at the bottom of the Empire State building, we agreed to meet for dinner at the end of the day at Kit and Liam's restaurant. I had never visited New York before and was keen to start my tour with a view of the city from the top of its most famous building. As luck would have it, however, our excursion into the clouds was tarnished by rain, renovations to the highest floors and... cloud.

Manhattan, with its noise and bustle, is very much an adult place. Tempted by Broadway and the clothes shops on Fifth Avenue, we decided instead to opt for a toy shop on Madison and give the afternoon to the kids. This place was unbelievable – it could only be in America. There was everything from fifteen-foot-tall King Kongs to miniature Mercedes sports cars – at $9,000 each, cheap at the price. Given the incredible range, I suppose I got off lightly in the end, when Jackie bought Kelly some costumes to dress up in and Daniel, to my great surprise, decided that what he wanted most was a ball.

As for myself (we're all kids at heart), I spent an hour in the joke department, looking for a gadget to catch someone out. I'm not sure whether it's a result of the sun or not, but practical jokes have been slightly down this time, compared to other trips.

Three summers ago, during a tournament we played in Boston, we got some great laughs out of this dummy can of beer that gave the most wicked electric shock when you picked it up. I remember we were in a bar one night when this poor old sod, stone cold and soaking wet, wandered in off the street and started begging for money for drink. The counter in front of us was lined with half-filled bottles, but when Aldo gave the guy the nod and told him he could take a bottle, the guy reached out for the make-believe can. As he picked it up and was greedily reaching for the ring-pull, it whacked him. 'Shiiit,' he screeched, throwing it into the air. Although we shouldn't have been laughing, we were absolutely splitting ourselves, because no sooner had he been duped than he was wrapping his jumper around his fingers, trying to pick it up again.

Searching for something along similar lines, I eventually settled for 'Flubber', one of these gunge-type things that goes 'puuuhhh' as soon as you stick your finger in. Not sure it will fool too many of my team-mates, I'll store it with the whoopee cushion I sometimes use on the FAI.

After the toy store, I raised my arm – New York City style – for a cab. Jackie wanted to take the kids on a horse and carriage ride around Central Park and in particular to show Dan, who is a big *Home Alone* fan, the section of the park in front of the Plaza hotel where Macaulay Culkin runs out and meets the old tramp (Brenda Fricker) with all the birds on her arm. The tour cost $34. We were shown Madonna's apartment, Demi Moore's apartment and the spot where Macaulay Culkin acted out his scene. It was half past five when the tour ended, and time to make our way to the restaurant for dinner. As we left the park we met an Irish supporter – one of many we have encountered while visiting the city.

Have you heard the news?' he asked. 'Do you know it's Holland you'll be playing and not Belgium?'

'You're joking.'

'No. Belgium were beaten by Saudi Arabia this afternoon, and Holland beat Morocco and top the group on goal difference.'

Thanking him for the information, I was surprised and pleased. I thought: 'Good. If we are going to play anyone in Orlando, we'll take Holland. I know we can handle them.'

The Cascarinos, Stauntons, McGraths, Morans, Kernaghans and McGoldricks were already seated when we arrived. Kit and Liam installed us on one of the best tables in the house, their hospitality almost a match for the view, which was quite out of this world – rush-hour traffic piling over the Brooklyn Bridge as one by one the giant buildings began to light up. It was a great night, and by nine o'clock we were only just starting to enjoy ourselves when it was time to leave. The children were tired, worn out, and the bus driver was waiting, so after thanking my cousins for a lovely evening, we marched outside, where some buskers were playing on the plaza. A beautiful water-side setting with these incredible buildings sparkling in the background, it was as if someone had painted a mural you felt you could reach out and touch. Rewarding each of the buskers with a tip – as one good musician should always do to another – I felt that if someone had handed me a chair and a couple of cans of Bud, I could have sat there all night.

Once on the bus, we asked the driver if he could take us on a sight-seeing tour.

'Where would you like to go?' he asked, sounding remarkably like Doctor Ruth.

'I don't know,' I replied. 'Anywhere – can you take us through the Bronx?'

'*You wanna go to the Bronx?*'

'Could we?'

'Wellll,' he replied, sounding worried, 'that's a shade too far from here. What about Harlem? I can take you through Harlem.'

'Okay, that would be great.'

Visually it was everything I expected it would be. There were people sitting out on the pavements, with three- and four-year-old kids still running around at eleven o'clock at night. We saw a car that had been set on fire, buildings with their windows smashed, walls sprayed with graffiti…. 'There's a shooting here once every ten minutes,' the driver informed us. The itinerary also took us to the Apollo Theatre – 'Everyone who is big in New York first started here' – and along the route John and Yoko used to take to Central Park. 'This is where he got stoned one night and wrote Strawberry Fields.' Listening, although I wasn't sure how accurate the driver's information was, I was loving every word of it and didn't really care.

Kelly was out for the count on my shoulder when we arrived back at the hotel, where a group of journalists ambushed me in the lobby. 'Have you heard about Maradona?' they asked, in unmistakably excited tones. That facet of human nature always amazes me. I mean, you can be at home and hear of the most appalling tragedy on the news and be bursting to tell your wife about it as soon as she gets in. Anyway, when they said this about Maradona, I thought they were going to tell me he was dead, had been killed in a car crash or something. When they mentioned he had failed a dope test I was surprised, but with Kelly weighing a ton on my shoulder, I was in no real position to say a lot else. Whisking her off to bed, I retired for the night myself. One of the better days.

The Lambeth Walk

HOLLAND
(JUNE 30 TO JULY 7)

 **DAY 25**

THURSDAY JUNE 30:

STRAWBERRY FIELDS

On the flight back to Orlando this afternoon, I was handed an eighteen-day-old newspaper, and although I'm not normally a newspaper person, I read every word. I'm missing newspapers, missing being up to date with what's going on in the real world. Back home I buy the *Sun*. Why? I don't know, because I'm much more intelligent than that. I suppose it's because their football coverage is good. I wonder what they printed about Maradona this morning? Nothing too complimentary, I suspect. It's a shame he should bow out so distastefully. Of all the footballers I have watched, he must rate as the finest. Blessed with God-given talent, he was able to do more with a ball than any other player on the planet. I'd place him right up there on a par with Pele.

I sat beside Charlie, our kit man, on the flight down. Although we give him dog's abuse, he knows we all love him and regard him very much as one of the boys. A former League of Ireland referee, he was telling me he was a wood machinist before he retired, which prompted me to ask him his age. 'Guess?' he said. 'Fifty-eight,' I stabbed, sure I was close to the mark. 'Try again,' he laughed, and after repeated failed attempts we eventually arrived at seventy. I couldn't believe it. Neither could Jack when I informed him later. He joked that he would have to have him fired: 'I can't have you at seventy running around after us lot! You'll keel over!'

'Naah Jack, it's no problem,' I offered in Charlie's defence. 'If he keels over we can just bung him in one of the skips to bring him home.' (Charlie's just about five feet tall.) Joking apart, he gets through a phenomenal amount of work, especially on a day like today when, with Mick and Larry Quinn, he'll shift tons of baggage and equipment. On the flight I asked him about work and the stress (*'Charlie! What are we doing in the wrong kit?'*).

'Wouldn't you sooner be sitting at home in front of the telly with a cup of tea?'

'Naah,' he replied, 'there'll be plenty of time for that.'

Cass has had a miserable time since he tweaked his hamstring in training the first week. Although he started back with some light work on Monday, the indications are that he will struggle to play a game. That's a real blow, considering that Chelsea don't want him and that he had intended to use the World Cup as his shop window. That's not to say he hasn't had offers. Every day a fax will arrive from a Reading or a Blackpool, and every day his morale will slip a bit further.... 'I can't believe this; I'm better than that.'

The ultimate blow came last week, when he received a message asking him to contact Mike Walker immediately. Thinking straight away of the Everton manager, he dialled the number and was put through. Walker was saying, 'We'd like you to come... we want to give it a bit of a go... because across the road Forest are....' And of course, as soon as he mentioned Forest, it suddenly dawned on Cass, who had been saying, 'Yeah, great,' all along, that he wasn't speaking to the Everton manager at all, but to Mick Walker of Notts County. Funny though it was, I felt too sorry for him to laugh.

Although we've known each other since the age of fourteen, it's only in the last five years that we've become good friends. From our beginnings together at Interfico, I went on to play for Welling United, Cass went to Crockenhill and we slowly drifted apart. As soon as I learned he had signed for Gillingham in the Third Division, I used to watch for his name in the results. Converted from centre half to striker, it was inevitable, once he began knocking them in regularly, that he would move to a bigger club. Still at Gillingham when I signed for Southampton, he moved to Second Division Millwall in 1987 and formed an understanding with Teddy Sheringham that would make them the most potent strike force in the English League.

The last four years, however, have not been kind – a dip that began, ironically enough, during the last World Cup. Having entered the tournament as an automatic choice up front, he exited it as the replacement to the promoted Niall Quinn. In March of that year, Graham Taylor had paid £1.5 million to take him to Aston Villa, but what should have been a golden opportunity sadly never worked out. Used to being supplied at Millwall, he became a supplier at Villa – a target man who laid the ball back for others in general, and David Platt in particular, to feed from. A marvellous finisher, Platt didn't always appreciate the simplicity of the square ball, and from being a twenty-seven goals per season striker, Cass found his quota suddenly diving.

A second million-pound move to Celtic a year later promised to turn that around, but the team was a poor one and again didn't play to his strengths. He was plagued by recurrent injury which affected his fitness, form and confidence as he considered another move, and suddenly his options had dried. It was as if overnight you could go from being a £1.5 million hot-shot to a player nobody rated at all. Aware of his frustration through our contact on the Irish team, I put in a word for him at Chelsea with Ian Porterfield, who had mentioned he was looking for a big man to play with Kerry Dixon up front. Luke-warm on the idea at first, Ian changed his mind after travelling up to take a look at him and a deal was done to bring him back to London.

The goal he scored on his Chelsea debut should have signalled a fresh start, a new beginning, but was soured by the booing he received as he ran out. He couldn't believe it. I couldn't believe it myself: no one deserves to take stick before they've had a chance, and it was totally out of order. Aware of how deeply he'd been hurt, I suggested that I might mention it in my column in the programme notes (I was club captain), but he didn't want to know.

The last two and a half years – again disrupted by injury – have been hard on him: just when it seems he's getting it together, some other niggle comes along. This latest, the calf injury, is an especially cruel blow. Niall's cruciate ligament problems should really have opened the door for him, but unless we make it to the final, I'm not sure he will make it back in time to play. Not normally the moody type, he's been a bit down of late and tonight, as a long-shot to turn his luck around, he phoned a clairvoyant faith healer in Orlando that Kevin had recommended and asked if she would come to the hotel.

'For God's sake, don't you go telling all the lads,' he urged when it was over.

'I won't, I won't. Now what did she say?'

'Well, she sat me down, and before I could say a word she said, "I can tell things haven't been going very well for you of late and that you feel you've been let down by people around you."'

'And what did you say?'

'Well, I said, it's not so much that I feel let down by people around me, but rather that I've let myself down a bit, although I've not had the best of luck, to be fair.'

'And?'

'"Well," she said, "all I can tell you is that things are going to turn for you and that those who doubted you will soon wish they hadn't."'

Sceptical, but not wishing to dampen this new lantern at the end of his tunnel, I said, 'Well, you never know.'

Talked to Jackie on the phone tonight. She has checked in with the children and the rest of the wives at the Marriott on International Drive. As for us, we're back in the good old Hilton in Altamonte Springs. Room 811 hasn't changed since I've been away, and out of sheer boredom this afternoon I slipped over to the shopping mall and bought myself a walkman and some tapes. I crashed out with it around my ears in bed this evening.

'Let me take you down 'cause I'm going toooo
Strawberrrry Fields....'

DAY 26

FRIDAY JULY 1:

DEDICATED FOLLOWERS OF FASHION

Jack wasn't on the flight with us when we flew down from New York yesterday. Convinced, like everyone else after our 0–0 draw with Norway, that Belgium's last outing would prove no more than a formality, he'd travelled up on a reconnaissance mission to Washington to watch them play Saudi Arabia, when where he really should have been was here, in Orlando, watching Holland beat Morocco. Bad weather and flight delays meant he didn't arrive back until the early hours of the morning – all of which might explain his foul humour out at the training ground.

After the warm-up, the opening exercise was the one where he splits the squad into three different queues, one on the right wing, one on the left and one in the middle. On Jack's nod, the ball is played out to the right or left wing, run down the by-line and then whipped across for the player who started it to finish. However, wilting perhaps under the strong sun, they weren't executing the move as precisely as Jack would have liked. And didn't he let them know! 'Noooo,' he bellowed. 'I want the ball driven across, not passed across. Don't pass it, just whack it across and make him get on the end of it.'

On any other day, I would have been out there taking an earful like everyone else but, excused from the session along with Jason (bruised rib) and Gary Kelly (blistered feet) because of my sore knee, I was pissing myself watching on the sideline. The expressions of terror were priceless. 'Well done Stan, good ball son,' I roared as the pitch vibrated under a fresh bollocking. For once it felt good to spectate.

The limousine was waiting when we slipped outside. Slightly delayed by the late return from the training ground, eight of us piled in and instructed the driver to take us to a place called Tamoquin. With a 'T' time reserved for a quarter to three (terribly efficient people, these hotel bellmen), we knew we'd be cutting it fine if we were to get back before raising any suspicions at seven. Kitted out as we were with clubs and buggies, getting out was a real problem. We drove from the first to the tenth, to the first, to the tenth, then back to the first, trying to work out which was the shorter queue. Then, just when we had decided it was the first, the starter decided otherwise: 'No, you guys, I told you. You have to go off on the tenth.'

'I know, we heard you,' I argued, 'but I'm not sure if the people in front are just pushing their buggies along or if they realise they've got to put their foot on the pedal to make them go, because they're so slow up there it's ridiculous.'

Eventually, however, we teed up and drove off. Playing for ten dollars a hole, myself and Dave Kelly took on Ronnie and Ray, while in front, Cass and Shez played Kevin and Denis. The rules were simple: in order to secure the dollars, both players had to win the hole – i.e. our best had to beat their best and our worst their worst. Dave and I started well and were two up after three holes. Ronnie and Ray were having problems. When one would make par, the other would get an eight, and it wasn't long before they began looking at each other, wondering when the other was going to start pulling his weight.

In the other four-ball up front, they were playing for the Crown Jewels, or so it seemed from the rate of their advance. Sizing up each putt from the front, behind and the side, Nick Faldo and Fanny his caddy wouldn't have taken as much care. Abandoning the round after fifteen holes when the skies opened, we led a convoy of buggies back to the club house. The limo picked us up as arranged at six thirty, and when we walked into the dining room at five minutes to seven, you would have sworn we had just jumped out of bed.

The goatee beard is in fashion. Roy Keane was the first of the team to sport one, but since coming out here, Aldo, Cass and Dave Kelly have each followed suit. Aldo's surrender to the latest trend surprised me, because he's an old-fashioned lad at heart. On the day we visited the hair salon two weeks ago when I changed my 'look', I tried very hard to get him to do the same. 'Go on,' I urged, 'have something different. You've had that little quiff on the top now for the last ten years – have the whole lot scalped.' But in the end he settled for the traditional short back and sides. It was a great surprise, therefore, to see him at the dinner table this evening with a diamond stud in his ear.

'Aldo! Are you sure?' I asked.

'Ah sod it,' he said turning around. 'I always fancied having it done.'

'Well fair play to you, son.'

As we were eating away, Kevin nodded across in his direction: 'I can't believe he's had that done.' And the more I started thinking about it, the more I had to agree. Curious, I got up and walked around behind for a closer look.... It was a magnet, a small but powerful magnet behind his ear that was holding on the diamond (fake of course). He hadn't had it pierced at all. Delighted at having drawn us in, he showed us a little box of them he had picked up in some joke shop.

Jack arrived.

'What do you think, Jack?' we asked, nodding towards Aldo.

'What's that in your bloody ear?'

'Had it pierced Jack. Yeah, you know, always fancied having it done.'

Jack looked at him, horrified. Kevin, meanwhile, had got his hand on the little box and slipped one on each ear, just as Conal Hooper, one of the team doctors, sat down.

'Can you actually get infected by having your ears pierced, doc?' Aldo asked.

'Ah, you've had your ear pierced, have you?' Conal replied, looking across.

'Yeah.'

'How did you have it done?'

'Well, I just got like... a badge and pulled the pin to one side and just like whacked it through.'

'And was it sterile?'

'Sterile?'

'The pin, did you sterilise it?'

'Well, I don't know... I wiped it on me shirt a bit first.'

'Well, unless it was sterile there's a high chance your ear will become infected.'

Across the table, we were having to work very hard indeed to keep a straight face. Smelling blood, Kevin picked up the chase. Sounding deeply concerned he asked: 'Is that right, doc? Seriously? Can we get infected?'

'My lord, yes. If you've done it that way, Kevin, then yes, you could well be infected.'

'Shit,' said Kevin. 'That's the last thing I need. What shall I do?'

'Well, I would take them out tonight and perhaps – as it's the first night you've had them pierced – leave them in a solution I can give you.'

Amazed at the doctor's naivety, we could no longer suppress our urge to laugh and the scam was blown. I mean, Aldo's would have thrown anybody, but Kevin is thirty-eight years old! The two gold sleepers in his ears were the sort of thing my four-year-old daughter would wear. Poor Conal, how on earth would we manage without him....

Monday's game is slowly beginning to creep into our thoughts. Rumours of dissension in the Dutch camp are encouraging. Koeman apparently has turned around and said he wants Rijkaard playing alongside him, and we've heard one or two rumblings that morale is not all it could be in their hotel, all of which has to be a plus for us. Although no one will admit it, secretly we are all daring to look beyond Monday to the prospect of a quarter-final against Brazil in Dallas. It's not that we don't rate Holland or that we're sure we will beat them, but their form so far in the tournament – coupled with our 1–0 defeat of them in April – leads us to believe we've got every chance.

Orlando's mosquitoes continue to feast on my carcass. I've been bitten on my legs, my back, my bum, everywhere. Add this to the rash that continues to bubble away under the surface of my knee (although in fairness that is getting better), and all things considered I'm a bit of a physical wreck. A few weeks ago, the combination of these ills would have left me pulling my hair out, but I'm past caring now. Four weeks in Orlando change your perspective on life.

SATURDAY JULY 2:

RUMOUR HAS IT

Every day starts with a rumour at breakfast. Yesterday, I was the victim.

'You do realise that if we draw on Monday, it's sudden death and not penalties?'

'No.'

'Well under the new rules [and there were plenty of them], from now on when the game goes to extra time, the first team to score wins.'

'Oh, I didn't know that.'

'Yeah, it's like over-time. And if there are no goals after fifteen minutes each, then it goes to penalties.'

'Crikey, that should be interesting.'

But it wasn't true at all. The day before, it was Eddie McGoldrick's turn.

'Eddie, have you heard about Darren Anderton?'

'No.'

'He's gone to Arsenal [Eddie's club].'

'What! Darren Anderton has gone from Spurs to Arsenal?'

'Yeah, they've just signed him – £3.6 million.'

'Ah well... that's me on me way then.'

Again, another load of crap. So this morning, when somebody mentioned that the Colombian Andreas Escobar was dead after being shot twelve times as he was leaving a Colombian restaurant, we didn't believe it; thought it was just the latest ridiculous rumour. For once, though, the rumour was true. We talked about it for most of the morning. Kev said that if it was a team-mate of his, he'd never want to play for his country again. Later, on the news, they showed a clip of his car and reported he had been shot because of the team's elimination from the tournament and his own goal against the USA. Can you believe that? It's crazy! I mean, supporters back in England and Ireland are passionate, and it sometimes amazes me the lengths they will go to in order to see a game, but this is bordering on the lunatic. An absolute tragedy for the team, his family and his friends.

We trained at the Citrus Bowl at midday. When we arrived, the Dutch were just finishing their session, and though we shouldn't officially have walked on until they had all vacated the pitch, we decided it was big enough for both of us. Aldo saluted Ronald Koeman on the way out – they know each other from Aldo's couple of seasons with Real Sociadad in the Spanish league.

'Ah, played in Spain have we? Know a few famous people, a few big names?' I asked, after they had finished their little chat. Then, turning to Gary Kelly, I said: 'Gary, why don't you go over to that Bryan Roy and invite him out for a bit of training so you can put him in your pocket again?' because he absolutely destroyed him last time in Tilburg. Gary just laughed.

The session, when it started, wasn't that strenuous: a warm-up, twenty minutes of shadow play up and down the pitch, some finishing with the goalkeepers and then an old 'uns versus young 'uns five-a-side which, much to Stan's disgust, the old 'uns won again. I went for a bit of a nap in the afternoon, nodding off during the Spain-Switzerland game. Spain are looking good at the moment – I've fancied them a bit right from the start and they could well be the dark horses of the tournament.

TV and video entertained us for the evening: drawn to the games room by yelps and screaming, I sat down with a few of the lads to watch *Miss Fitness USA* which, if you ask me, should have have been called *Miss Steroid USA,* because although one or two of them looked naturally fit and healthy, it was the ones with the massive shoulders, the chiselled chins and square jaws who went forward to the final rounds. Still, it kept the lads amused for an hour, and as scantily clad hulks flexing their biceps on the cat-walk are not my cup of tea, I went and broke my record – 404 million – on the pin-ball machine. Later, we watched a *Billy Connolly Live in LA* video for what must have been the zillionth time, and tonight I went to bed with some Jon Bon Jovi around my ears...

> You want commitment
> Take a look into these eyes
> They burn with fire,
> Until the end of time

...it took me a while to go to sleep.

DAY 28

SUNDAY JULY 3:

PASS THE CHEESE

The second round being knock-out time, today's session out at the Seminole County training ground finished with penalty practice. It's a waste of time really, because when you remove the pressure of a packed stadium and a couple of million television spectators from your shoulders, slotting them home is the easiest thing in the world. But when it's for real....

❀   ❀   ❀

Genoa: Monday June 25, 1990
With ten minutes to go to the end of extra time, we had to face the inevitable. One hundred minutes of play had failed to break the stalemate between Ireland and Rumania, and whether we liked it or not, the visa to the quarter-finals of the World Cup was about to be decided by penalties. We eased down in those final minutes, and when the ref eventually blew, we shook hands, wished each other well, then retreated to separate camps on either side of the centre circle.

The selection of the 'five' was interesting.

'Who fancies one?' asked Jack as we passed the bottles around. Kevin Sheedy and Ray were obvious choices. I'd been taking them all season for Norwich, so my name went in as well. Dave O'Leary, surprisingly, seemed almost keen to take one, which made four – but then we began to struggle. Mick (McCarthy) didn't fancy one; Quinny didn't fancy one; Paul didn't fancy one; Chris Morris didn't fancy one. Aldo, whom we normally entrusted with our penalties, had been replaced in the second half by Cass, and Steve Staunton – another 'automatic' – by Dave O'Leary.

'Are you a man or a mouse?' Ray asked Cass.

'Pass the cheese,' Cass replied with a grin. We had our fifth.

The break between the end of the battle and the start of the war was short and not very sweet. As I stretched and tried to loosen my limbs, my stomach began to tighten. We were almost ready now. The ref ordered us to pull our socks up and put our shin pads back on. (The risk of contracting Aids while playing sport was pretty topical during the last World Cup, and although I've never heard of anyone being infected by a hairy shin or pad, I believe that was the ref's concern.)

This was not going to be fun. The Rumanians won the toss and with it the psychological edge of shooting first. Hagi stepped forward. Packie guessed right, but Hagi's shot was high and hard and brilliantly struck. One–nil Rumania.

Kevin Sheedy, one of our bankers, was first up for us. As he placed the ball on the spot, I studied Lung, the Rumanian keeper. In order to give themselves some sort of chance, keepers like to dive that split second in advance. Which side would Lung choose? The left? The right? He chose his left: Sheeds pinged it straight in the middle. Then Lupu made it 2–1 to Rumania.

Ray stepped forward for us. 'Get your heads down and whack 'em,' Jack had advised during the interval, but Ray, I knew, would try to place it. Having sent Lung the wrong way, he sank to his knees in delight: 2–2. When Rotariu made it 3–2 for Rumania, it was my turn to step forward.

I'm not sure how many yards it is from the centre circle to the penalty spot, but it felt a very long way as I walked down. So many things can go through your mind at moments like that – the enormity of the stakes, the millions watching as you step toward the dice – but I tried to block them out. Bluff, you see, is half the battle. Placing the ball on the spot, you want to appear cool, confident. You want to take three paces back and say, 'Blow that whistle, ref, because I know exactly what I'm doing with this,' when in reality you are absolutely trembling.

Placing the ball on the spot, I knew exactly where I was going to hit it. I stepped back, didn't take my eye off the target. 'Christ, this Lung is a big fellow,' I thought. 'If he goes the right way he'll save it.' But then, just as I started my run, he crouched, making the target suddenly bigger. I hit it cleanly, side of the foot, aiming for the left-hand corner, then held my breath as Lung dived... to the right. Goal: 3–3. I turned round, blew a huge sigh of relief and walked back towards the lads in the centre, where Ray inquired with a laugh whether I needed a change of shorts.

The screw was tightening with every kick. Lupescu was next up; Packie almost got a hand to it. At 4–3 to Rumania, all eyes focused on

Cass. Walking down, he looked like a man who was about to be shot by firing squad. He placed the ball, ran up and tried to blast it to Lung's left, but stubbed his toe in the turf on impact. Lung guessed correctly and almost got down in time – but had to watch in agony as it whistled under his arm-pit.

'I don't think they'll be able to fill the hole I've just created in that penalty spot,' Cass joked when he came back. 'It must be about a foot deep.'

Was it Cass' crater that put Daniel Timofte off? Who knows? What I do know is that the tension was absolutely unbearable as he stepped up to take Rumania's fifth and final penalty. If he scored, all the money in the world wouldn't have tempted me into Dave O'Leary's boots. However, Packie was getting closer with every kick, and the supporters behind his goal – all Irish – wound the heat up even more. Timofte ran up, aimed to slot it to Packie's right, but had to watch in agony as it was brilliantly turned around.

Unable to contain ourselves, Cass and I sprinted down and dived all over Packie, only to be sternly reminded by the linesman that there was still one penalty left. With the score at 4–4, Dave O'Leary had to win us the game. From the moment he stepped forward, I never doubted. Incredibly cool where others would have buckled, he made no mistake and slotted it home. As I joined the stampede to congratulate him, the sheer joy of that moment was stronger than any I had ever experienced in my career… but I don't want to go through that again tomorrow. No, sir. I'll settle for a straight 1–0 win.

MONDAY JULY 4:

THE LAMBETH WALK

08:30 Mick raps on the door. Another day, another dollar, another step towards our goal. This morning I feel like the greatest left-sided midfield player in the world. I feel this because Mick Byrne has told me so and Mick Byrne never lies.

'You're the greatest thing on two legs,' he tells me. 'Nothing can stop you when you are playing well. Nothing can stop our team. Today we're going to cut through the Dutch like a knife through butter. We're on our way – the impregnable green machine.'

He's an amazing fellow: a motivater, physio, mother, shoulder to cry on, the focal point of all our jokes…. The thing I love most about him is his passion for the team. Myself and Cass wind him up something chronic. Once last year before an international in Dublin, having checked to see that he was out in the corridor, I let out a scream for him to come to the room.

'*Miiiick.*'

'What's up, what's up?'

'Have a word with Cass.'

'Why? What's wrong with him?'

'He says he's going to retire from international football.'

'Whaaat!'

As we were talking, Cass was standing by the side of his bed, putting clothes into his bag.

'I'm sorry Mick,' Cass said. 'I can't keep doing sub to Niall. It's doing my head in. I've had enough – I'm going to tell Jack.'

'You can't tell Jack. Don't be silly. Are you mad? You're a great player, son. You can't do that.'

'No, it's come to the crunch. I'm off.'

'You bloody well won't retire… over my dead body.'

And with that we both dived on him and slapped him around the chops.

08:45 It's a midday kick-off today. Three hours doesn't give you much time to sit and worry about a game. The last time we played Holland 'for keeps', four years ago in Palermo, it was different. With a 9.00 p.m. kick-off, the build-up that day was one of the longest of my life. We got up, had our walk, ate lunch and then Jack sent us to bed for the afternoon. We were staying in a small, family-run hotel, where the rooms were hot and the air conditioning poor. Needing at least a draw if we were to proceed to the next round, we were too tense to sleep and congregated instead in the small reception area downstairs.

We played cards, sipped coffee, read every word of every paper, did all the crosswords and by mid-afternoon were bored out of our minds. Mick, getting worried by the length of our chins, said, 'Aldo, Ray, come on, cheer up.' But with six hours to kill before kick-off Aldo and Ray weren't interested: 'Piss off, Mick. Leave us alone.'

'Cass? Andy? Cheer up.'

'Shut up, Mick. Leave us alone.'

So then, in honour of the two of us, he started singing: 'Any evening, any way, when you walk down Lambeth Way….'

Now, although the hotel was plain enough, the reception area was decorated with these magnificent model ships, each standing on its own marble plinth. And as Mick broke into song, he performed this little jig to accompany the words.

'…you'll find us all…'

Watching from our position on the sofa, it became obvious to us…

'…doing the Lambeth Walk…'

…how unaware he was of how close he was to one of the largest of the ships behind him.

'…Oy!'

As he iced the cake with the 'Oy', he shoved his elbow back and tipped the model off its ledge.

What followed was pure pantomime. Lunging desperately to catch it, he managed to get his fingers to it, but couldn't stop it shattering on the solid marble floor – and as it did, Mick's expression changed from one of joy to complete horror. As the hotel manager raced to the scene of the disaster, we rolled around in our seats, kicking our legs and holding our bellies for fear they would explode.

'Why you break my boat?' the manager, visibly upset, demanded in his broken English.

Mick was as white as a sheet. 'I'm sorry. I'm terribly sorry. I didn't mean it. No mean it. Accident. Accident.'

'Why you break my boat? Why you break my boat? You crazy,' the manager insisted, then turned to his wife and began ranting in Italian at 300 miles an hour.

'I'm sorry, I am genuinely so sorry. It was a complete accident, I....'

But then the wife joined in, throwing her arms up and giving it hot and heavy to Mick. For five minutes he stood there and took it on the chin, until finally he snapped and decided he wasn't taking any more. Pointing to the manager, he said, in his broad Dublin accent: 'I no sorry with you any more. Fuck you and fuck your boat.' And with that he stormed up to his room.

As he said it, we were all fighting for air, trying not to wet ourselves. It was like something you'd see on *Fawlty Towers* and would certainly have strolled the ten grand award for best in the series on *Beadle's About*. When I followed Mick up to his room, we sat on the edge of his bed and just roared. He couldn't have done anything better to have broken the monotony of the afternoon.

09:00 Not much time for monotony this morning; eat your breakfast, distribute your tickets and then step from the hotel to the bus. I am feeling fine. Outside, the day is warm but cloudy. Inside, the mood in the camp is good. I think we all genuinely believe we can win the game.

10:00 'Come on lads. We've been out here for four frigging weeks. Enough is enough, let's get home,' Aldo jokes on the coach. We sit at the back. He seems in good form and is hopeful he will be playing, because he has always done well against Koeman in the past. 'One night in the Nou Camp [stadium in Barcelona], I gave him a real run-around, slaughtered him. The way to play on him today is not to give him any room, to stand on him and let his mate knock it around.'

10:40 We arrive at our dressing-room, put our bags down and walk out on to the pitch to take a look. I like a little walk on the pitch before a big game – it's a good way of getting your adrenalin to pump. Jack calls me over for a word while we're out. 'I'm going to play Gary Kelly at right back today. And Tommy, Ray and Stan.' Unsure of whether he wants my opinion on this, I nod 'okay' and we walk back in. Should I mention the conversation I had with Aldo on the way to the ground? Perhaps. Would he change the team if I did? I don't know. With less than two hours to kick-off, there doesn't seem much point in sowing doubt in his mind.

10:50 When we walk back in, he names the team: Packie Bonner, Gary Kelly, Paul McGrath, Phil Babb, Terry Phelan, Ray Houghton, Roy Keane, John Sheridan, Andy Townsend, Steve Staunton and Tommy Coyne. We change, run back out for a bit of a warm-up, and when we come back in, he gathers the five midfielders around him for a little chat.

'We're playing to win, and today we need to run at them a little bit more – but I expect us to keep our shape. Roy, I want you to do your anchoring job. Ray and Steve, when you get the chance to get in behind them, do it, and do it early.'

11:00 Four years ago in Italy, the build-ups seemed more tense. Maybe it was the evening kick-offs, maybe it was the passion of the Sicilian crowds... I don't know. Whatever it was, there were definitely a lot more nerves in the dressing-room. Things seem much calmer the second time around. I have a shave. Some of the boys play cards. When the buzzer sounds for us to go out, I feel good and strong – not leggy and lethargic as I did against Mexico. As we walk out, the atmosphere doesn't compare to the fire-cracker buzz of New York. Maybe it's the heat, or the weariness of travelling up and down, but when '*Come on ye boys*' starts ringing around the ground, it seems to lack the intensity of other games.

12:00 Both teams start positively – so positively that my earliest thoughts are that the game will be a cracker, for it is truly end to end. Then, unfortunately, we begin making mistakes. The problems start with Koeman. When we played them earlier this year, on a beautifully cool evening in April, the conditions enabled us to hustle and run all night, and Koeman couldn't lift his head but there was a green shirt bearing down on him. With him unable to pick out his passes, our back four were able to push up really tight, and in the end we ran out comfortable winners.

Orlando's heat and humidity, however, make it more difficult to play the running game and to exert that sort of pressure. With Roy dropping off to stop the supply through to Bergkamp, Jonk is being given far too much room in the middle of the park. So is Koeman, whose forty- and fifty-yard passes are putting our back four under all sorts of pressure and making it impossible for them to get tight. Doing unto us what we had done to them, he nearly puts Bergkamp through a couple of times with clever little chips over the top, and in the tenth minute, when he plays another in behind Terry Phelan, we are suddenly in big trouble.

12:12 The ball bounces high, awkwardly. Taking a gamble in heading it back, Terry can't get enough power on it and is caught flat-footed as Overmars seizes the opportunity. He can only watch in horror as the Dutchman takes it to the by-line and casually knocks it across for Bergkamp to slot home. As setbacks come, it is pretty major. I mean, sometimes, when you concede a free kick on the edge of your box and the ball is smashed at one hundred miles an hour into the roof of your net, there isn't a lot you can do about it. But when you concede one through a basic error, it is a particularly cruel blow. Still, it happens to the best of us and with nearly eighty minutes to play, the cause is far from lost. 'Come on lads,' I urge. 'Keep going. Let's not chase the game; let's not go mad.'

12:41 A very unusual thing happens just before they strike again. Wallowing in the space in the middle of the park, Jonk takes a ball from either Rijkaard or Koeman and accelerates past John Sheridan. As he tees himself up for the shot, I am thinking, 'Shoot. Please shoot. Go on, hit one. Hit one from there,' because nine out of ten attempts from that distance out either don't hit the target or are easily saved. So he shoots, he hits one – straight at Packie Bonner, who takes his eye off it for a second, lets his hands drift apart and allows the incoming missile to slip agonizingly through his fingers.

12:42 Glancing over towards the bench, I can see they are visibly shocked. I am shocked myself, but with just three minutes to go before half-time, this is no time for panic.

'We've got to get the back four up; we're too deep,' John Sheridan says to me as we walk back to restart play.

'Yeah, I agree with you,' I reply. 'But we've three minutes left in the half. Let's sort it out at half-time.'

12:50 There are no accusing fingers when we go in. No pound of flesh sought from Packie or Terry. With Jack, the time you know you'll get a bollocking is when you err and get away with it. And he's right. I mean, when you make a cock-up and they run through and score, you don't have to be reminded that you should have cleared it into the stand. You've asked it of yourself at least a hundred times. No, Jack is relatively calm and wears that same 'What can I say to you?' look he wore when we walked in at Lansdowne Road last October, three–nil down against Spain.

Wary that I'm possibly stepping on toes, I decide the time has come to make a case for a change of strategy. 'Jack,' I say, in front of everyone in the room. 'You've got to put Cass on. You've got to put Cass on, because if you do I know what will happen: Rijkaard will drop back into their back four, because the others won't be able to handle him [Cass], and with the change, we might be able to get at them. We've got to play 4-4-2.'

But Jack won't wear it. 'I can't put him on. I would be... he's only done two days' training in a month and I don't think he will last the half. If I put him on and his calf goes again after twenty minutes and I have to pull him off again after twenty minutes, then that's knackered me. It's killed me. Bugger that. We'll have to see how it goes.'

I then mention Koeman, who's been picking out passes as if he's playing in a practice game. One of his side's 'big players' in many ways, he is also their weakest link. Catch him on the ball, for example, and he will never recover – he's too slow. Our problem is that we haven't got near him to rush him. Turning to Phil Babb, I say, 'Phil, if Rijkaard is there and I've run at Koeman, then you step in and pick him [Rijkaard] up. We might as well let Macca [Paul McGrath] pick up Bergkamp, let Gary pick up that Van Vossen guy and let everyone go a bit man-to-man. We've got to start pressing them a bit to make things happen for ourselves.' And in the second half we do.

13:00 As the game restarts, I still feel we can turn it around. If we can get one back early on, I feel we can win before extra time, but although we try our nuts off, it isn't happening for us in front of goal. I keep looking across at the bench, waiting for another of our strikers to come on – Cass or Aldo or both of them. But I know the way Jack is thinking. Football is a funny old game. Two–nil is a funny old score. If we can claw one back, we'll suddenly be right in the game, but to let one more in would be The End. Ten minutes into the half, I begin to sense 'one of those days'. Our shooting from outside the box is terrible and slowly the game is slipping away.

13:30   Cass comes on and does very well in the air for us, but by now we have used so much energy chasing the game that we are knackered, and it is becoming harder and harder for us to stay in touch with him. When the balls are banged up to him, he's nodding them down, but he only ever has one player with him, whereas on a wet night at Lansdowne Road he would have one alongside him, one running past and one looking for him to lay it either side. We do, however, have a couple of chances: Jason whips a ball across, I whack it first time with my right and feel like it's whistling towards their net – until it hits Koeman in the belly, the first time we've caused him discomfort all day.

13:45   The final whistle sounds more definitive than usual. Rijkaard looks knackered, out on his feet. I shake his hand and wish him luck in Dallas. 'I hope you go on and do well,' I offer. 'I wish I was going home and going on holiday,' he replies. I'm not sure he's joking.

The left back de Boer also offers me his hand. With five minutes to go, we had a bit of a run-in, when I threw a drinking bag and hit him in the face. I'm not sure what made me do it: Maurice Price had just thrown it to me from the touchline and, biting into it, I tried to swallow a mouthful but was too knackered to finish it. De Boer was standing a couple of feet away and, as I say, for reasons that are still unclear to me, I decided to let him have it flush in the gob. A few people in the crowd booed – quite rightly so, because it must have looked terrible.

'Sorry about that,' I apologise.

'Good shot,' he laughs, seeing the bright side. He is right, it was a good shot – my only one on target all bloody day.

13:50   In an odd way, these minutes saluting our fans on the pitch now it's over are probably the ones that will stay with me most a couple of years from now. This is my final curtain as far as the World Cup is concerned, and I could have walked around and done two or three laps just clapping and waving to our fans, who once again were brilliant. No team has been better supported in America, and I hope one day we can win something for them. In the stand I spot Jackie, Daniel, Kelly and my brother Mike. When I shrug my shoulders at Jackie, I can see

THE LAMBETH WALK 183

she has been crying, and there are more tears in our dressing-room when eventually we leave the field.

Four years ago, when we walked in at the same stage of the World Cup having beaten Rumania, we were all sobbing. 'We're going to Rome,' cheered Mick Byrne then. 'We're off to see the Pope.' What a great moment that was.

Things are a lot more solemn this time. Jack comes in. There are no inquests. He shakes the hand of every one of his twenty-two players and thanks them individually for their efforts along the two-year path to where we are standing now. As I watch the exchange of hands, it suddenly dawns on me that it really is over and I feel quite sad.

Packie is still visibly upset about his error in the first half. As he sits there with his head in his hands, one by one we try to gee him up and one by one we fail. We all know exactly how he is feeling, and while it is easy for people to say, 'Don't worry about it,' you do worry, you do care. I've missed penalties in my time. I've run up, blasted it over the bar and thought, 'I can't believe I did that.' It's the outfield players' equivalent of letting the ball slip through your hands. Naturally the type who would feel he had let us down, Packie has made a fine contribution over the four games and has no reason to feel ashamed.

15:00 A buffet is laid on when we return to the hotel. We sit around, have some food and the afternoon gradually fades into evening and then night. Cass' old sparring partner, Teddy Sheringham, joins us at the bar when the 'wake' is in full flow. He can't get over the singing and good spirits of the Irish supporters and the way they are mingling with the players as if they are the best of pals. 'This is special all right,' he says. 'Can you imagine standing here amongst English fans after we had just gone out of the World Cup? They would probably want to have a go.'

21:00 The group has already started to splinter. Alan McLaughlin and Eddie McGoldrick are home flying this evening. Tommy Coyne leaves tomorrow. I'll probably stay with the team at least until Wednesday, but won't be accompanying the official party on the flight back to Dublin. Pre-season training resumes at Villa in a couple of weeks and we haven't had a holiday, so I'm going to fly up to Boston with Jackie and the kids to stay with my brother for a few days.

Four years ago, the break-up after our quarter-final defeat was different. We were transported in an open-top bus from Dublin airport to the city centre, people pouring on to the streets in their thousands in a spontaneous gesture of thanks. Before today's game, there was talk that the 'homecoming' was to be repeated, only this time on a grander scale to allow supporters to participate in comfort. A giant stage was being erected in the Phoenix Park and some bands were being hired, but today's defeat has put an end to all that – we think. We're not sure. One minute it's on and the next it's been cancelled. It's all very confusing. Tonight, I've made up my own mind. There's not a lot of summer left; I'm off to Boston.

DAY 30

TUESDAY JULY 5:

THE MOURNING AFTER

For four years now we've been a team: Jack and Maurice; Mick and Charlie and Larry Quinn; Kevin and Aldo and Ray and Packie; Stan and Shez and Cass and Denis; Roy and Kells and Paul and Ronnie and Terry and Alan and…. For four years now, we have looked towards the same horizon – the World Cup – to boldly go where once we had gone before. We lost some friends along the way – Big Mick, Dave O'Leary, Sheeds, Chrissy Hughton, Chris Morris – and found some talented new faces in Phil Babb, Alan Kernaghan, Gary Kelly, Jason McAteer. But essentially, the core of our group remained the same.

For six weeks now we've been a team. For six weeks we've lived by the same clock, shared the humour, lived by the same routine of sleep, train, sleep, game. All for one and one for all: 'Come on, lads. Let's raise it a bit.' 'Come on you boys in green.' For six weeks now we've lived the life of rock stars. Tea and toast in the morning? McDonald's at midnight? Our wish was someone else's command. Orlando today, New York tomorrow. For John Aldridge, Andy Townsend and Kevin Moran read John Lennon, Jon Bon Jovi and Leonard Cohen. 'First we'll take Manhattan, then we'll take Berlin…' except that we won't be taking Berlin. We're out. It's finished, over. Strange how abruptly it has all come to an end.

There's been an incredible sense of anticlimax about the place today. A couple of the lads played golf. I lazed around and did some shopping with Jackie, and couldn't help but be struck by how deserted the hotel lobby seemed when we got back. Most of our supporters are making their way home; the television crews and press have followed the Dutch on to Dallas. It felt odd not to be ambushed by a microphone or an autograph book.

Yesterday, as I walked around the pitch after the game, I didn't have any tears in my eyes or lumps in my throat. Although it was probably my curtain call as far as the World Cup is concerned, I didn't feel all that emotional. Waving to our supporters, the message I most wanted to impart was: 'Thanks, you've been marvellous. We've all enjoyed having you here with us; it's been great.' Today, however, as reality begins to permeate, there are times when I feel quite sad.

Talk at dinner was of future plans. Kev will probably retire (although I wouldn't bet on it). I'm not sure what Paul will do. Aldo will return and score another hundred goals for Tranmere, but as to whether he will pull on another green shirt for Ireland again, he's not sure. As for myself? Well, while I would like to think there are some talented left-footed Brownes from Castleisland waiting to take my place, I hope I can at least hold on until the European Championships.

We also talked about the homecoming. It's on again, and after a couple of conversations with Ray – 'If some are going back, I think we all should' – and Mick, I've decided to return tomorrow with the team.

DAY 31

WEDNESDAY JULY 6:

HOMEWARD BOUND (PART ONE)

17:30   Take-off. I can't say I'm sorry to be leaving Orlando behind. I just wish this was a direct flight. With two hours on Kiwi Airways to New York, then six or seven on Aer Lingus to Dublin, it promises to be a long day's night.

18:00   Four years ago, on the day we flew back to Dublin, some baggage handler at Rome airport rifled my bags. Indeed, as I write, he is probably chasing a ball around the cargo area with his mates, with either Donadoni's, Koeman's or Mark Wright's shirt on his back. He wasn't, however, a completely heartless bastard and left me with my Egyptian shirt. If he ever gets to read this, I'd just like to say, 'Thanks, mate.' For the last three years, Ismail El-ha-la-who-la-ha's shirt has really looked great on my wall. Once bitten, this morning when I packed my suitcase, I decided I was taking no chances and would carry my souvenirs as hand luggage. I included one of my green shirts as well and sent Daniel around my team-mates on the flight to have it signed.

19:00   Looking back on the tournament, I'm not sure if I enjoyed it quite as much as last time. Italy, four years ago, was a voyage into the unknown for us all – players and supporters – which only Jack had experienced before, and it was always going to be different second time around. Looking back on the games, while I'm sure we could have played better, I'm not sure we could have given more. The opening game against Italy was a dream start, a massive start. Whatever it was about that game, we just felt confident right from the off – not that we were going to win it, but that we could come away with a draw.

The Mexican game, ironically enough, was supposed to be our 'banker'. That, of course, was before we travelled out here and experienced the drain of the Orlando heat. We were always going to struggle once the thermometer passed the eighties and Mexico, in fairness, were perhaps a better side than we gave them credit for. The Norway game was disappointing. We could have beaten them, should have beaten them, but there's not a lot you can do against a team that doesn't try. Then, against Holland, we conceded two soft goals and were always chasing the game. Eliminated from the competition one step shorter than last time, while we achieved what we set out to achieve overall (to qualify for the second phase), after such a brilliant, brilliant start, the end was a touch disappointing.

The problem we have as a team is that there is nothing hidden about us: what you see is what you get. Not short of brave, hard-working triers – and I include myself in this category – what we lack is that split second of individual brilliance that can give a team an extra dimension and instantly turn a game. The Italians, for example, can call on the Baggios of the world; the Brazilians on the Bebetos and Romarios. We are what we are, and while we will never be far away, you need a bit more to win tournaments like this.

19:30   How will I look back on my Ireland years? What will be left of a relationship that seems so special now with the Irish people? I'm not sure. I know, in the eyes of many people, I will never be looked upon as a true Irishman, as a Kevin or a Packie or a Ronnie, and I understand that, because I'm not – I have Irish blood in my family. But in ten years' time, when people remember the team, I hope there will be a place for me somewhere. If they said nothing more than, 'He always gave his best,' that would please me no end.

20:00   Switching terminals at JFK, I am struck by the folly of fame and sport. Five weeks ago, when our flight touched down from Dublin, we were whisked to a waiting coach and given a police escort to our connection on TWA. Tonight, we have to ask a cleaning lady for directions on how to reach the Aer Lingus terminal by foot. It's a funny old world.

21:00   Takeoff again. Kelly is exhausted and falls asleep on my shoulder. A few of the lads are playing cards; I sip a beer and take a read of the Irish papers. Although the night will be short, I can't be bothered to try and sleep. I want to go home.

DAY 32

THURSDAY JULY 7:

HOMEWARD BOUND (PART TWO)

07:30 'Right,' says Michael Morrison, an FAI official. 'I just want to give you a few plans about what happens when we land. Everyone is going to leave the plane via the exit on the right, except the players and senior FAI officials who will exit the plane on the left. The wives will be driven directly by coach to the hotel. The players will proceed across the Tarmac to a small reception with the Taoiseach, Albert Reynolds.'

I look at him. 'Fine, no problem.' This is my first mistake. Jackie is sharper.

'I've got to be honest with you,' she tells me. 'Why do we have to go out the back door? I mean, I'm not looking to go down the stairs first, but I'd like to be with you. And I'd like your kids to be with you.

I know she's right. I should stand up here and now and say, 'Sorry, but my wife and my children are coming down with me at the front.' All it would take would be for one of us to make a stand and the others would follow suit. But I'm tired and irritated and this whole home-coming business is starting to weigh me down, so I say nothing. This is my second mistake.

08:00   When the door opens, the FAI officials are quickest down the steps. There are television cameras everywhere and a fine crowd has turned out. We give them a wave, shake a load of different hands and are led to a reception, where a presentation is made to Jack. Whisked to the Airport Hotel, we shower, shave and are instructed to change into our suits for the short helicopter hop to Aras an Uachtarain, the home of President Mary Robinson. I'm beginning to wilt now with tiredness, and while it's an honour to be in her company, I'm not sure if I can actually remember anything she says.

12:00   The stage they have built in the Phoenix Park is like something from a U2 concert. Marched on to the platform, we are introduced to the crowd and then interviewed by Pat Kenny and some other guy from

RTE. Not nearly as big a turn-out as four years ago, it was great given the timing (the middle of a working day), and it's a nice experience for Gary and Phil and Jason and Roy, who didn't experience it last time. People, surprisingly, are very sympathetic – 'Ahhhh, I think it's very unfair you've had to cancel your holidays to come back for this' – which seems odd, given that we have been pressurised into thinking they are the ones who want us back. Could it be that there are hidden agendas at play here? It certainly seems that way.

16:45   Eddie Corcoran has booked me four seats to Heathrow, where Jackie has left the car. Given our state of fatigue, she argues that perhaps it would be wiser to stay in Dublin, but I can't face another night in a hotel. More than anything else in the world, I just want to go home, put my suitcases down, close the front door and shut out the world.

18:00   Reclaiming our luggage from the baggage hall at Heathrow, we load up two trolleys and wait for a courtesy bus to take us on the twenty-minute drive to the car park.

   'Are you going to be all right to drive?' Jackie asks, as I slip the keys into the ignition.

   'Yeah, I'll be fine,' I assure her.

20:00   Fifty miles to Birmingham – almost there. We stop for a cup of tea at some services, where I'm recognised by some children as 'the guy who played in the World Cup'.

   'It makes me laugh,' I say to Jackie. 'They're probably Arsenal or Man United fans. In a couple of weeks' time, when they realise I play for Villa, they'll probably hate my guts.'

21:00   Thirty-one hours after leaving the Orlando Hilton, we arrive in Sutton Coldfield. Daniel and Kelly are unconscious. I carry them up to bed, empty the boot of the car and at last arrive at that moment I have been waiting for. 'Sorry, world, but I'm checking out for a while.' I close the hall door.

DAY 33

FRIDAY JULY 8:

ALL'S WELL...

It's the simple pleasures you miss most – tea in a mug, Teletext, toast. One of the things I most disliked about America was the axle grease they served for butter, so this morning, when I got up, I couldn't wait to slap some good English butter on a bit of hot toast. It felt great to be free from room 811, to be able to walk with the dog in the park, sit around and strum my guitar, mess around in the garden with Daniel, and do nothing really.

I can imagine how some of the other lads would have spent the day. While Ray would have jumped up and said, 'Right, where are my golf clubs?' Stan would have been much more laid back. He'd have slept all morning, then nipped down to his local in Dundalk for a pint in the afternoon. Yes, it's the simple things you miss most, like jumping into the car with your slippers on to drive to the newsagent's, so you can hand over your 20p for a copy of the *Sun*. I skipped pages one to twenty-seven and read the three sports pages in about two seconds flat. Some things never change.

The call came late this evening.

'Guess what?' Cass challenged, sounding very pleased with himself.

'What?'

'Someone's come in for me?'

'Yeah? Who?'

'Have a guess.'

'Oh, go on.'

'No, have a guess.'

Aware, given his excited tones and the little charade, that it's obviously someone decent, I reeled off a couple of the Premiership clubs.

'No, no. It's abroad.'

'Is it really? Well then, you'll have to help me out and give me a clue.'

'It's France.'

'Not... Marseille?'

'Yeah!'

'You're joking!'

'Nah, straight up.'

'Brilliant, mate! How did it come about?'

'Well, because of all the messing around [bribery scandal] last season, they've been relegated to the second division and prohibited from buying any new players. Which is where I come in, because they can get me on a free [transfer].'

'And? Go on. Carry on.'

'Well, yeah. I've made a couple of calls and they're interested and the money is good – so I'm flying over to Paris in a couple of days to thrash it out with Monsieur Tapie.'

'Crikey! That's brilliant, mate. Good luck to you, son. Now go out there and prove them all wrong. You couldn't do something for me, could you?'

'Yeah, sure. What?'

'Go check in your bag and see if you've still got the number of that faith healer you met in Orlando. I think I'd like to give her a call.'